CRUSH SCHOOL
STUDENT GUIDE

Learn Faster, Study Smarter, Remember More, and Make School Easier

PROPERTY OF

_____

Published by Focus 2 Achieve
www.focus2achieve.com
Minneapolis, MN
1st Edition, July 2018 by Focus 2 Achieve.

ABOUT THE AUTHOR

Oskar Cymerman is a teacher, writer, and a Chief Creative Engine at Focus 2 Achieve, and educational media and consulting company.

He blogs and trains on brain-based learning, personal improvement, professional growth, and peak performance at _focus2achieve.com/blog_ and for other outlets including Entrepreneur, Teaching Channel, and Bam Radio Network.

His articles and books focus on teaching kids, teens, and young adults success skills. His goal is to empower parents and teachers to help their children learn how to learn and acquire new skills using smarter, faster, and better methods.

Oskar's favorite clients are academic organizations and innovative forward-thinking organizations in need of professional development on teaching and learning new knowledge, platforms, and skills, and peak performance.

For workshop inquiries email him at _oskar@focus2achieve.com_.

BONUS: Grab the FREE ebook version of Oskar's previous book
Crush School 2: 10 Study Secrets Every High Schooler Should Know
bit.ly/f2asignup

Oskar's Other Books Available on Amazon:

Crush School: Every Student's Guide To Killing It In The Classroom.

The Power of Three: Simplify to Amplify.

TABLE OF CONTENTS

TABLE OF CONTENTS CONTINUED...

INTRODUCTION: WHAT YOUR LEARNING & STEPH CURRY HAVE IN COMMON

Contrary to popular belief, becoming a better student is not about spending a lot of time reading books, watching videos, or filling out worksheets. It's about knowing how your brain works and using it the right way. And most importantly, crushing it at school and in life is about putting in *smart* time, not *more* time.

Let's look at a famous underdog story of the Golden State Warriors 3-point machine Stephen Curry to illustrate the point of putting in *smart*, not *more* time. The Chef, as he is often called was picked 7th in the 2009 NBA draft, following 6 players of which only Blake Griffin and James Harden consistently grace the NBA highlight videos. The other 4 turned into busts (2) and role players (2). But because Curry was considered somewhat undersized and unathletic he was passed over by 6 teams. "Story of my life," he'd say, but let's examine what it took for Steph to crush it in basketball.

To learn how to play, you have to understand how to shoot the basketball so it has a chance to go into the hoop. Then, you have to do it over and over to master the right technique - the grip, the spin, the shooting motion, the footwork, and so on. Then you use the technique continuously in practice and during games. Simple enough, right?

But here's the deal. Learning what the shooting technique is supposed to look like is easy. Learning how to shoot, on the other hand, can be hard or easy based on how you approach it. Someone can show you and walk you through the shooting technique step by step and you can grasp the idea in under 3 minutes. Pretty great, right?

It is. But it's not enough. Not even close because you know you have to take it a step further. You have to do it. You have to shoot the ball. Once? Nah. Twice? Nah. You have to practice the shot over and over. You can do that for say 15 minutes if you have some success and don't get bored. And you might even learn to shoot okay this way. But there's a better way. A way you might have not considered. A smarter way. A way that lets you reach the elite level faster. All you have to do is know and use this smarter, faster, and better way.

The better way consists of two things: Deep Understanding and Mastering the Micro Skills. Let's discuss the microskills (a set of smaller skills that combine to form a big skill) that make up the skill of shooting the basketball.

If you have a good coach (mom, dad, brother, friend, gym teacher etc.) he or she will break the shot down into smaller skills. First, he might ask you to focus on the right way to hold and support the ball. He might do this by passing you the ball 20 times, each time checking how you adjust your hold and correcting it if needed. You're not shooting yet, just practicing how you hold the ball over and over quickly. After you do it right 10 times in a row quickly you move on to the next thing.

The coach shows you the shooting motion and how to spin the ball. He stands 5 feet away and you "shoot" the ball, not toward the basket but to him. Slowly at first so he can make the necessary corrections and talk about the ball's arch, you pick up the pace until you master doing it fast. Then, he might move further away and ask you to do the same thing. After a few minutes of that, he's moving around - forward, and back, and to the sides. Later you work on getting the jump on your jump shot just right. When that's all done you get the test. After mere 10 minutes of running different drills it's time to shoot for real.

You stand 5 feet away from the hoop. You shoot and make the first one, and then the second, and then you miss. After 20 shots, you're 13/20 - 65 percent. Then you shoot from 10 feet out, hit 55 percent, and 45 % when 15 feet away. Each time, your coach gives you feedback on the micro skills you practiced *moments* earlier. You won't be as good as Steph at threes or even shooting but you've cut down on the time it will take you to get to that level because you've built a platform you can now build on top of. The fundamentals - the bball shot micro skills are there for you to review and apply to make more shots tomorrow, next week, whenever.

Alternatively, someone could tell you how to do it and you could have spent 15 minutes *just shooting* - spending time rebounding, running after and picking up the ball, resetting your feet, hands etc. - instead of isolating and practicing the micro skills first and receiving feedback from your coach. Now ask yourself: *Which way is better?*

Stephen Curry wasn't always a great shooter but at barely 30 years old he's considered the greatest shooter ever by many basketball experts. He was so small in high school that he had to change his shot to outplay the bigger players. So, helped by his father, Steph worked on changing his release point to avoid his shots being blocked by his opponents. This switch took a month-and-a-half during which he was so bad that other players started asking why he bothers playing basketball.

Ray Allen still holds the record for most made three pointers. That number stands at 2,973. Allen, an outstanding 3-point shooter, was 38 years old and in his 18th NBA season when he sunk that 2,973rd 3-pointer. The Baby-Faced Assassin will reach 3,000 in his 12th season as a pro and before his 33rd birthday. Assuming he plays into his late 30s, by the time he hangs up his Curry 5s (or more likely 12s) Steph would have crushed the 3-pointer record.

And now it's time you apply the same principles to school and crush it too. How do you do that?

First, you must understand the tools you have at your disposal - your brain and how it works. This will give you the power to start making decisions that help you get the most out of your brain - just as Steph figured out how to play the game he loved with what he had. Being undersized and less athletic than many other players, he understood that he must use a unique approach to become a great player. Thanks to this approach, he routinely "outskills" everyone he shares the hardwood floor with.

And this brings us to the second ingredient that will help you crush it in school: skills. Specifically, understanding and consistently using a variety of effective learning micro skills is what will help you reach the level at which you can learn anything teachers throw at you. And because you will learn smarter you will learn things faster, understand them better, and remember them longer. Steph the Chef did exactly the same - he worked on developing a skill set that allows him to create opportunities and consistently make shots from beyond 22 feet and 9 inches. And he will continue to do that for years to come.

But there's a wrinkle. To know how to study smart, learn things faster, and improve your school success, you will have to learn many of the micro skills - the learning strategies that work - on your own. The good news is the strategies are common sense. The bad news? They're not commonly taught in schools.

The problem with schools is that most teachers expect you to "shoot treys" with Curry-like efficiency before giving you the chance to be Charles Barkley. Sir Charles was a great player with terrible 3-point stats eclipsed only by an atrocious golf swing. And we want you to know all the micro skills before you show up in our class.

Here, I want to apologize for that and explain. You see, teachers suffer from the curse of knowledge. We are older and our brains are more experienced and prepared than our students'. We know our subjects well. Teaching the same stuff over and over, we tend to forget how learning all of it was like. Trust me when I say that many of us were confused at school many times.

We also feel obligated to cover the curriculum. It's like a mad race to the finish line and we forget that learning, real learning matters most. As a result, we often don't allow enough class time to explain and practice the microskills you need. We give you homework instead. I'm sorry for that.

We don't break down the concepts or the skills enough in english, science, and math. We assume too much. We don't coach you enough during class. We move on too quickly. Learning is often superficial.

You don't remember skills or information taught in class. You are left to learn on your own. Not having the right platform - a set of effective learning strategies and understanding how they benefit your brain - you frequently use crude devices such as rereading or flashcards to memorize facts and pass tests. A few days later you get a grade and forget "its" from "it's." I'm sorry for not doing more to "make it stick."

Teachers teach concepts but not the way to master and remember these concepts. We don't teach many of the micro skills of learning effectively. We might tell you how to take good notes and advise you to use spaced practice. But often, we assume you already "have a system" and your shortcomings are due to lack of effort. This may sometimes be the case but it's not like we followed you home to see how much time you spend studying.

So, it's up to you to come up with a system; a better way that works for you. When interviewed by ESPN once Stephen Curry offered this advice:

"As you evolve, it's almost like a game within a game. When you get to college, then the pros, everything resets and it's an equal playing field. You've got to figure out how to differentiate yourself. You've got to figure out how to get to a certain level and how to stay there. The time you put in is what will determine that."

Let's be honest, Steph was modest and said "certain" level instead of elite "level" where he clearly is. You've got to put learning time and practice time in to become elite at learning, but the smarter you use that time the faster you will get there and the faster you will learn.

It will take you **25 hours or less to cover all the micro skills** in this guide. It will take you **longer to learn them.** But if you use these micro skills consistently, learning them will happen on its own.

Knowing many learning strategies and having multiple options for learning will give you the knowledge and the confidence you need to become an advanced learner. But to become an advanced learner, you will have to use these strategies because knowing them does little for your success. If you complete all the activities but keep using the old strategies that haven't worked so well, you'll be exactly where you started.

No matter what the discipline, most people stay average or crash out. Only a few achieve greatness. To achieve greatness, Stephen Curry learned the skills and practiced them. He's still practicing them. Once in practice, Steph made a ridiculous 77 three-pointers in a row. When he missed number 78, he grabbed Draymond Green's jersey and screamed. He made 94 out of 100 three-pointers during that practice drill.

Thus, using what you know and challenging yourself to do better every time is the difference maker.

This book is your coach. Use it well.

See you on the other side.

PART 1:
BUILDING A BETTER PLATFORM

What Is Part 1 About & Who Is It For?

Consider the evolution of transportation.

For over 200,000 years, humans walked, climbed, or ran from point A to point B.

Then, somewhere between 5,000 - 10,000 years ago we jumped on backs of horses and let them take us places. Later, we build carts and carriages for the horses to pull.

And then, a little over 100 years ago Henry Ford said "If you think you can do a thing or think you can't do a thing, you're right" and he built *Model T*, the first car. It cost $850 and reached the top speed of 45 mph, which is faster than a horse but slower than a cheetah.

And now, the Tesla Roadster can exceed 250 mph and will set you back 200k. Suddenly point B got a lot closer. Actually, it's the same distance away but you can get there a lot faster now. Except, no road can handle the speed and the power. Aside from a few testing facilities and race tracks, no platforms exist to handle the Tesla Roadster. Just as a regular road is the platform needed for a regular car, the right road is the platform necessary for this supercar to showcase its full potential.

But what does a Tesla Roadster have to do with learning and why should you care?

Simply put, human brain is like a supercar. YOU HAVE THE POTENTIAL TO BE A TESLA. But right now, your ability to learn effectively is made up of both Ford Focus and Mercedes parts. You're good at some things and unaware of others. But, regardless of how good or bad at learning you are, you can become a Tesla Roadster. Not because I know you - I most definitely don't - but because I understand what the human brain is capable of and I know how to build a solid platform you can build your learning skills on.

This learning platform is a set of realizations and skills anyone can build to become a better learner. To start building a solid platform, you need to understand how the human brain works - how it encodes, stores, and retrieves information effectively. Then, you make the platform stronger by learning and using the basic but often disregarded skills. Many of these skills are simple but increase your learning results profoundly.

The lessons included in Part 1 of this workbook are designed to give you the foundation all your future learning will happen on. Skim through lessons 1 through 26 in Part 1 and decide what you already know and do consistently and which skills you still need to gain. Then, complete the lessons it contains. At the very least, focus on the lessons that teach you things you don't yet know to gain new skills. If you are confident that you have the skill a certain lesson teaches skip it. Move on to something you can use.

Remember that just doing the lesson is never enough. It's the consistent use of the skills you learn about that will help you learn how to use these skills to learn everything else, and make the biggest difference in school and life. To maximize your results - to Crush School - apply the skills you learn right away and keep using them when you're learning math, science, english and many other subjects the educational system decided to overwhelm you with.

Most importantly, you will be asked to create graphics, videos, drawings, summaries, and other products that may seem silly. Except they're not. Doing them will help you understand, apply, and remember the things you're learning. Remember the last time you read something and then did nothing? Of course you don't. Well… maybe you remember the act of reading. Too bad you don't remember what you read or learned. Actually, you learned nothing. Got it?

Crush school by building a learning platform you will be able to stand on your whole life.

LESSON 1 - COMPETENCE CREATES CONFIDENCE

BIG QUESTIONS

1. Why does competence create confidence?
2. How do you become competent at something?

QUICK COLLABORATION

1. With a partner or in a small group, discuss what the statement *"Competence Creates Confidence"* means to you. Give each person 30 seconds to talk and record their thoughts below.

My partners' thoughts on *"Competence Creates Confidence:"*

_____

_____

_____

_____

2. Now, have each person use another 30 seconds to explain how competence is created. Record below.

_____

_____

_____

_____

SHORT READING - Underline the statements you find important

"Competence Creates Confidence"

But what is *Competence* exactly? How do you get it?

Think about something you are good at, maybe really good at. Maybe it's a sport like soccer or basketball. Maybe it's painting, sculpture, or another art form. Maybe you're good at fixing stuff or cooking or gaming or have some other skill you feel *competent* in. How do you feel when you do stuff that requires you to use this skill?

Chances are whatever your mind conjured was positive. You feel good to do stuff you're good at because you experience success in it. This motivates you to keep going. You keep doing it and as a result you keep getting better at it. You keep getting better because once you feel competent you have the confidence to try new things. You try new ways; new techniques and strategies. Some don't help much but some lead to small improvements. Over time, this series of small improvements adds up to a big improvement which you likely don't even notice because you enjoy doing this thing you're good at so much.

Imagine school being this way. You might already be a good student but how would you feel knowing that no matter what subject you have to take you can crush it? How would you feel to have the confidence that you can understand difficult concepts, learn them fast, and actually remember them months later when it's final exam time?

Continue reading on the next page →

You see, there are 2 types of people in this world - those who fear change and let their anxieties paralyze them to keep them stuck and those who fear change but decide to face their anxieties and grow as individuals. The first type stays comfortable but average (or less than) while the second type of people succeeds at school, work, and life. The good news is that everyone has the potential to be successful.

No matter how good or ugly your present school competence is, you can get much better at school. And don't worry - you won't have to drink the weird Kool Aid to get there. All you have to do is follow the same process that took you to the level of competence and confidence you have in the other skills you're good at. Except this time it won't be trial-and-error. You will have small, easy, and specific strategies at your disposal.

You already have the "school skill." It's far from perfect but it's a skill and as such it can be improved. The only way to improve it is to change how you approach school - learn and apply new learning techniques and study strategies - things that help you do school smarter, faster, and better.

You see, after overcoming the initial anxiety of trying something new you will realize that it's the new experiences and new learning that lead to an upward spiral of success. As you get more comfortable doing things outside of your comfort zone, you end up learning even more, being more competent, and feeling much more confident. This is a result of the "happy" brain chemicals such as dopamine, oxytocin, and serotonin your brain produces when you experience positive feelings such as joy, confidence, or feeling successful.

Once you accept and understand that fear-induced stress chemicals like cortisol and adrenaline are normal brain reactions to all things unknown, you will lessen their effect on your decision-making. They will no longer prevent you from venturing into the unknown. It will become easier to start making small changes to how you do school and other life things. Each small change will bring more competence and more confidence and reduce stress while increasing the happy chemicals. Keep at it and you will become more than a great student - you will turn into a learning machine - someone who learns and applies new things to make their life better every day.

So, you've reached a decision intersection. You can go straight, left, or turn right. Here's what awaits:

Straight: Do nothing. Keep complaining. Stay as you are. Complain some more.

Left: Try to change. Study more. Grind it out. Do somewhat better at school.

Right: Learn and apply skills that help you learn faster, study smarter, and remember more. Improve your learning skills in small, easy steps that make you a much better student and school much easier.

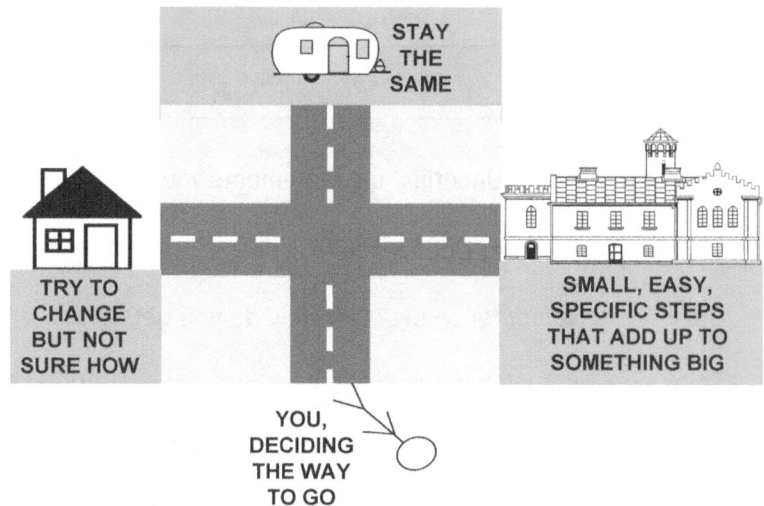

The **Right** decision involves change, which involves *Uncertainty*, which involves *Facing Your Fears*. But, it *Creates Competence* which *Creates Confidence*.

But you already know that. It's time to choose who you want to be.

SUMMARY - Look over the statements you underlined. Pick 2 and explain why you find what they say important.

LESSON 2 - SETTING ACADEMIC GOALS

BIG QUESTIONS

1. Why is achieving goals difficult? What prevents people from achieving their goals?
2. How will making SMART goals help you achieve them?

SETTING GOALS

Research proves that people who set goals for themselves are more successful than those who wing it. Thus, if you want to become a better student, you should set academic goals for yourself, write them down, and review them. They're like targets. If there's no target, you can't hit it.

My Academic Goals for This School Year

Write down 3-5 academic goals you would like to accomplish. Make it challenging but realistic.

1.

2.

3.

4.

5.

Why would you like to accomplish these goals? How will they improve your life?

QUICK COLLABORATION:

In a group or team of 2, discuss things that might prevent someone from achieving their goals. List them below.

SMART GOALS VIDEO

Go to **bit.ly/goalsmart** and watch the video on setting SMART goals. Take notes below.

S is for _____, which means _____

M is for _____, which means _____

A is for _____, which means _____

R is for _____, which means _____

T is for _____, which means _____

REWRITE YOUR GOALS AS SMART GOALS

Take the goals you wrote down on the previous page and make them SMART. Ask for help if needed.

1. _____

2. _____

3. _____

4. _____

5. _____

REFLECT

Write a short paragraph reflecting on what you learned today. Look at the BIG QUESTIONS at the beginning of this lesson and answer them.

_____

_____

_____

_____

_____

_____

LESSON 3 - LITTLE THINGS DONE CONSISTENTLY LEAD TO BIG RESULTS

BIG QUESTIONS

1. How can making little changes have a big effect on learning?
2. What are 2-3 little changes I can start making today to start becoming a better learner?

DAILY CONSISTENCY = MASSIVE RESULTS VIDEO

Watch the first 3:33 of the video *Daily Consistency = Massive Results* by going to **bit.ly/compound_it**. Pay attention to how the idea of compound effect relates to doing little things consistently.

VIDEO TAKEAWAYS

Discuss in a group how you could use the compound effect to benefit your learning. Explain below:

_____

_____

_____

ASSESS YOURSELF

In the table below, list all the things you do that impact your learning *positively* and all the things you do that have a *negative* impact on your learning.

Things/Habits I Do That **Help** My Learning	Things/Habits I Do That **Slow Down** My Learning

REVIEW YOUR SMART ACADEMIC GOALS

Review the SMART academic goals you created in the previous lesson, because it's time to divide them into smaller, more achievable steps.

MAKE IT SMALLER

One of the main reasons we fail to achieve our goals is that they seem to big and our mind becomes overwhelmed. This is why it's important to make the big goals smaller and split them up into smaller steps or chunks such as projects, tasks, or habits that get us closer to achieving the big goals. Use the table below to break up your academic goals into actionable things you can do every day.

Big Goal (write each of your SMART Goals below)	What are some good **habits** that could help me in achieving this goal?	What are a few smaller **projects** I could do to help me achieve this goal?	What are some daily **tasks** I could do to help me achieve this goal?
1.			
2.			
3.			
4.			
5.			

LESSON 4 - ACTIVE READING

BIG IDEAS

1. Why is active reading superior to passive reading?
2. Describe 5 or more active reading strategies you can use to remember more of what you read.

5 ACTIVE READING STRATEGIES FOR TEXTBOOK ASSIGNMENTS VIDEO

Go to *bit.ly/activeread* and watch 5 Active Reading Strategies for Textbook Assignments Video. Answer the questions and take notes below as you watch.

Take Notes	Make Notes

SUMMARY:

ACTIVE READING

Read *Chapter 13: Previewing* and *Chapter 25: Reading Tips* from the book *Crush School* below. Read actively. Here's the way:

1. Preview all headings, subheadings, bold text, and images.
2. Read the text taking notes in the margins and white spaces. Include only the most important information and stick to 2-3 notes per page only.
3. Immediately after you finish, write a short (2-3 sentences) summary of what you learned.
4. Put your phone in airplane mode. Set a timer to 15 minutes and begin.

{START OF READING}

Remember that movie preview you just saw?

Did it make you wonder how cool some parts of the movie will be?

Wasn't it awesome?

Previewing is a very effective movie marketing strategy. It makes you think and it peaks interest. It's because your brain is looking for connections it already has and makes new connections related to the topic.

Previewing awakens imagination, so use it! And it's easy:

1. **Before Reading:** Read the chapter title and all of the headings and subheadings. Examine pictures, charts, graphs etc.
2. **Lecture:** If the presentation is available to you ahead of time take a few minutes to skim it. If not, but you know the topic, find it in the textbook or online and give it a quick look before class.

Previewing will do 3 awesome things for you:

1. Your brain will look for information it already has in storage on those topics before you read/listen.
2. You will know what's most important and focus on it more while reading/listening.
3. You will remember more of what you read/hear.

And yes! To crush school (and life) YOU WILL HAVE TO READ.

Reading is often the difference between the haves and the have nots; those who succeed and those who are stuck in the same place.

To be able to take a piece of text, extract it's teachings, and apply them in many contexts is true power. It's the sort of power that gives rise to ideas, creativity, and innovation.

And, it helps you crush school too.

Let's talk movies for a bit. Ever notice how when you watch a movie the second time you find that you missed some things? Reading is the same way, so commit to reading whatever you're reading at least two times.

YOU HAVE TO READ A PIECE OF TEXT MORE THAN ONCE TO GET MUCH OF THE INFO.

Continue reading on the next page →

And, if you *actively* read the same text the third time, you will notice that you get more out of it still. The tips coming up will help you get really good at remembering and understanding. Ready?

HAVE A SYSTEM = GET THE INFO.

I don't know about you, but I often space out when I read. It's not that the book is boring. Sometimes I get into the reading and start analyzing what the author says in my mind. And my mind goes places. All of a sudden, I catch myself reading the words on the page, but thinking about Scarlett Johansson.

Does that happen to you? If it does, here's a trick you can use to keep focus and get the info.

WRITE IN THIS BOOK.

What?!?! But, my teacher said... Blah! Blah! Blah! Don't worry. I don't give detention and you won't owe me $87.50 for damaging the book.

IT'S YOUR BOOK, SO USE IT TO HELP YOU.

Yeah. I know it's pretty and all, but still

MARK IT UP!

When you do that, you focus better, remember more, and can find the most important stuff quicker the next time, which builds up your understanding. Check it out!

1. Underline or highlight key statements in each paragraph. This is the important stuff, not the info that supports the main points.
2. You are probably overdoing it if you highlight/underline more than ⅓ of the page. Just sayin'...
3. When you read a section the second time, take a few notes in the margins on WHY WHAT YOU READ IS IMPORTANT. Process, then write.
4. Next time you come back to the text, focus on recalling and writing deep study questions on the underlined information and margin notes.

If you absolutely can't markup the text take Active Notes (next lesson) or Cornell Notes on Steroids (*bit.ly/f2acornell*).

READING SUMMARY - Write a 3-4 sentence summary based on your understanding and your notes in the margins.

_____

_____

_____

_____

_____

_____

_____

LESSON 5 – ACTIVE NOTE TAKING

BIG IDEA

1.   What are the elements of active notes and why is it important to make meaning out of your notes?

EXAMINE AN INFOGRAPHIC

Go to *bit.ly/f2anotes* and examine the infographic. Take notes on the 7 elements of awesome notes.

Element #1 is _____ It involves _____

_____

Why does it work? _____

Element #2 is _____ It involves _____

_____

Why does it work? _____

Element #3 is _____ It involves _____

_____

Why does it work? _____

Element #4 is _____ It involves _____

_____

Why does it work? _____

Element #5 is _____ It involves _____

_____

Why does it work? _____

Element #6 is _____ It involves _____

_____

Why does it work? _____

Element #7 is _____ It involves _____

_____

Why does it work? _____

5 MINUTE BRAIN BREAK

Go to *bit.ly/cncnotes* and listen to the **Kwik Brain Podcast: How To Take Notes For Rapid Recall**.
Use the **Take Notes / Make Notes** strategy below as you listen to the podcast. The **left side is for paraphrasing** what you're hearing. The **right side is for making meaning** out of what you're learning.

Take Notes	Make Notes

SUMMARY:

LESSON 6 – MEET YOUR BRAIN

BIG QUESTIONS

1. How does the human brain learn and remember information?
2. What are the physical processes that happen in your brain as you're learning?

HOW TO GROW YOUR BRAIN VIDEO

Watch the video *How to Grow Your Brain* by Khan Academy by going to *bit.ly/brain_vid*. Pay attention to things that grow your brain, because you will have to draw a diagram representing this growth.

CREATE MEANING

1. Draw a diagram in the space below showing how your brain grows below.
2. Add labels, descriptions, arrows etc. Make it as detailed as possible.

3. Compare your diagram to those of two to three other people.
4. Make any adjustments and additions to your drawing above based on the discussion with your peers.

ACTIVE READING

Read *Chapter 4: Your Awesome Brain* from the book *Crush School* below. Read actively. Here's the way:

1. Preview all headings, subheadings, bold text, and images.
2. Read the text taking notes in the margins and white spaces. Include only the most important information and stick to 2-3 notes per page only.
3. Immediately after you finish, write a short (two to three sentence) summary of what you learned.
4. Put your phone in airplane mode. Set a timer to 15 minutes and begin.

{START OF READING}

Your Awesome Brain

The human brain has 100 billion neurons, each neuron connected to 10 thousand other neurons. Sitting on your shoulders is the most complicated object in the known universe." - Michio Kaku

WARNING! This part will be a little heavy on neuroscience, but it is important that I talk about what happens in your brain so you believe that **YOU CAN LEARN ANYTHING.**

If after reading this part you see it as nerdy gibberish than you are probably correct. After all, I specialize in nerdy sciency things.

But before you completely dismiss it know this:

I AM YOUR FATHER.

Okay. That's a lie. But still… Take a brief look at neurons and synapses on the next page, because I want you to know how great your brain is and what it does.

YOUR BRAIN IS AWESOME.

IT DOES AMAZING THINGS.

IT MAKES SENSE OUT OF NONSENSE.

EVEN GIBBERISH.

BUT YOU MUST GIVE IT A CHANCE.

Continued on next page →

Each brain cell or neuron you own has two main parts: cell body and axon. The cell body is the orange part with tentacles (kinda) called dendrites and axon is the red tail that also ends in tentacles (blue) called axon tips or terminals.

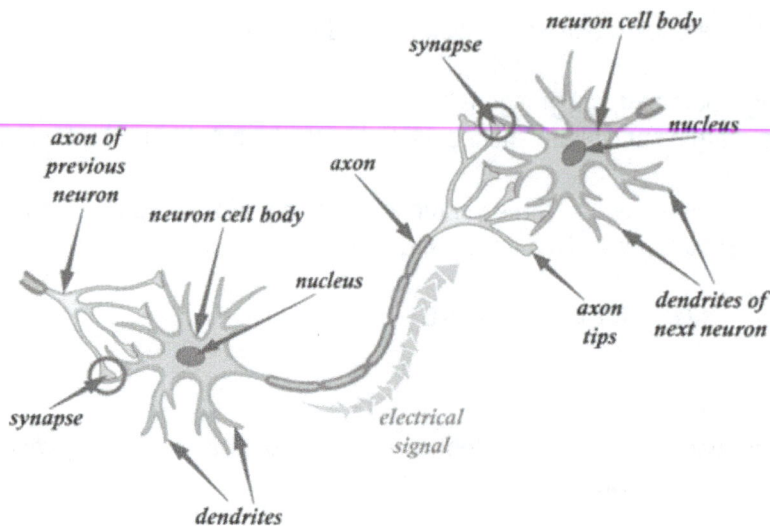

A synapse forms when axon tips of one neuron meet the dendrites of another neuron. When you are learning new concepts, new synapses form. Because the information is new the connections are weak at first.

Thus, the key to becoming an expert, a Jedi master at science, math, spelling, writing etc. is using the new information so the connections can become strong.

And, it matters when, where, how, and how often you use it. The more you do with the information the better you remember and understand it.

You see, **the brain is a use it or lose it organ that needs time to strengthen new connections**. Let it.

READING SUMMARY - Write a three sentence summary based on your understanding and your notes in the margins.

_____

_____

_____

_____

_____

_____

QUICK COLLABORATION:

1. Compare your summary to another student's.
2. Explain to each other which information you deemed most important and why.

REFLECT

Write a short paragraph reflecting on what you learned today. Look at the BIG QUESTIONS at the beginning of this lesson and answer them.

_____

_____

_____

_____

_____

_____

_____

LESSON 7 - ACTIVE LEARNING

BIG IDEAS

1.   What's the biggest difference between passive and active learning?

ACTIVE READING

Read *Chapter 14: LEARN ACTIVELY* of the book *Crush School* below. Here's how you read actively:

1.   Preview all headings, subheadings, and bold text.
2.   Read the text taking notes in the margins and white spaces. Stick to 3-4 notes per page only.
3.   Immediately after you finish, write a short (2-3 sentences) summary of what you learned.
4.   Put your phone in airplane mode. Set a timer to 20 minutes and begin. Do not stop until finished.

{START OF READING} Crush School Chapter 14: Learn Actively

Active learning is all about staying uhm… active.

Whether during lectures, reading, discussions, or watching videos, the key to getting the most out of these activities is to keep your conscious mind involved.

For example you might just sit there and hear the teacher talk or mindlessly watch a video in class. You'll remember something, but not much. So if you really want to learn this stuff you have to do something with it.

You see, the most efficient way to learn is to use the information right away in several ways. You're already at school a third of each day, so you might as well use that time to save time later.

And when it's time to study for a test, there are better ways than repeatedly re-reading notes or chapters. The table on the next page lists passive and active learning activities in and out of the classroom.

Check it out!

Passive Learning	Active Learning
Waiting for the Teacher to Teach	Previewing Notes or Before Reading
Listening to Objectives	Writing Objectives Down
Watching a Lecture	Taking Notes During a Lecture
Copying Text Word for Word	Thinking About and Paraphrasing Text
Highlighting/Underlining Text	Taking Notes in the Margins
Putting the Notes Away Right Away	Summarizing the Notes
Re-reading Notes to Study	Recalling Notes
Watching Others Solve Problems	Testing Yourself
	Asking Questions
	Making/Correcting Your Own Mistakes

And don't worry if some of the active learning activities are unclear right now. We will talk about them.

The key thing is that you know that in order to remember and understand what you are learning better, you have to allow your brain to process it and make meaning out of it. When you sit and stare at the teacher blankly or space out while reading a chapter, you're acting like a vegetable or a zombie.

There are many zombies walking around you. They sleepwalk through their classes hoping the information will magically seep into their brain. Then they complain when it doesn't. But not you. You learn actively, because zombies are only cool in movies. Or when they're in love.

SUMMARY - Write a 2-3 sentence summary based on your notes in the margins and what you learned.

_____

_____

_____

_____

ASSESS YOURSELF

Go back to the previous page and put a **V** next to each Passive Learning Strategy you use and an **X** next to each Active Learning Strategy you do not use.

Look at the **Vs** and the **Xs** and reflect. Are you more of an active or a passive learner? _____

Explain why _____

_____

What are some things you need to keep doing? _____

_____

What are some things you need to improve? _____

_____

5 MINUTE BRAIN BREAK

RESEARCH ACTIVE LEARNING STRATEGIES

Go online and research 3 active learning strategies *not mentioned in the reading* you can use to remember and understand concepts better. Name and describe them below.

STRATEGY #1: _____

This strategy involves _____

_____

It is effective because _____

_____

STRATEGY #2: _____

This strategy involves _____

_____

It is effective because _____

_____

STRATEGY #3: _____

This strategy involves _____

_____

It is effective because _____

_____

REFLECT: Write a short paragraph reflecting on what you learned today. Look at the BIG QUESTIONS at the beginning of this lesson and answer them.

_____

_____

_____

_____

LESSON 8 - LEARN FASTER WITH F.A.S.T.

BIG QUESTIONS

1. What can you do to learn faster?
2. What will you personally do to improve your learning?

EXAMINE THE F.A.S.T. INFOGRAPHIC

Go to *bit.ly/learnitfaster*. Examine the *F.A.S.T. infographic* and complete the chart below with *explanations* and *examples*. Don't copy mindlessly. Paraphrase and you will remember better.

F is for…
A is for…
S is for…
T is for…

ASSESS YOURSELF: Look at the chart you filled out and answer the questions below honestly.

Which single area of F.A.S.T. do you struggle with the most? _____

What are those struggles specifically?

_____

_____

_____

What is the one thing you can change or improve that will make the biggest difference?

_____

Make a plan. How can you improve it? What will you start doing differently? When will you start?

_____

_____

_____

5 MINUTE BRAIN BREAK

QUICK READING: THE *KISS* METHOD

Keep It Simple Stupid!" That's what my favorite teacher in High School, Mr. Dennis used to say. Besides being an awesome teacher, dude had a point:

WE TEND TO OVERCOMPLICATE THINGS.

Don't feel bad if you do it, because it's human nature.

Multitasking is one way we make a mess of things.

Do you have friends who tell you they want to hang out, but rarely do? They mean well, but stuff always comes up. They are pulled in so many different directions, they end up forgetting or not having time.

In reality, they get less done, because they try to do everything at once. They are a well meaning hot mess. Typically, they don't even realize it.

Basically, when you multitask you split your attention between different tasks and end up being less efficient and less productive.

Cardigan and suit wearing ninjas (psychologists and other scientists) have done experiments that showed:

1. Multitasking sucks (I read it in an article).
2. We get stuff done faster doing one task at a time compared to switching between tasks.
3. The more complex the tasks, the worse our performance and bigger the time waste when multitasking.

It's time to dump multitasking.

COLLABORATE TO ELABORATE

Discuss the key point of the article in a small group.

REFLECT

Write a short paragraph reflecting on what you learned today. Look at the BIG QUESTIONS at the beginning of this lesson and answer them. If you are ready to change the way you do something, commit to it here.

_____

_____

_____

_____

_____

_____

_____

LESSON 9 - MOVE & FEED YOUR BRAIN

BIG IDEAS

1. Why and how does movement and exercise help your brain perform better?
2. What are 10 foods that help you have a healthier and sharper brain?

ACTIVE READING

Read *Chapter 2: Move* from the book *Crush School 2* below. Here's how you read actively:

1. Preview all headings, subheadings, and bold text.
2. Read the text taking notes in the margins and white spaces. Stick to 3-4 notes per page only.
3. Immediately after you finish, write a short (2-3 sentences) summary of what you learned.
4. Put your phone in airplane mode. Set a timer to 15 minutes and begin. Do not stop until finished.

{START OF READING}

In case you haven't noticed, this book talks about the brain a lot. But then, this here chapter is about movement. And since it's not good to move your brain, because concussions really suck, let's talk about moving your feet and other parts and how that helps your brain, which helps your thinking, which helps your learning.

The story begins with Sir Craven Caveman craving a meal. He ate everything there was to eat around his cave and found himself starving. He wasn't that smart at the time, but by sheer luck, or more likely thanks to a powerful survival instinct, he realized he had two options. One, die. Two, move and find food or die trying.

Both options had a high risk of death associated with them, but the second option at least promised a few thrills and possibly offered survival. Lucky for you and I, Sir Caveman ventured out, undoubtedly collected a few bruises along the way, and walked, ran, and climbed his way to survival.

I know. You're probably like *What does some dumb cave dweller turned wanderer have to do with me? I can get my fried chicken, nanas, and coconuts at the store!*

You're right, but... When Sir Caveman left his comfy cave and started hustling in the hood, his brain became bigger.

He was discovering new surroundings, dealing with which required more brain power. He encountered entirely new things. He had to make sense out of them to decide whether he can use them, or if he should run from them. The deadly things were bigger, stronger, and faster than him. To survive, Sir Caveman had to be smarter.

Each day, he was running, climbing, and jumping to avoid, protect, gather, and kill. He was learning how to survive, and ultimately thrive, in new, changing, and hostile environments. He was doing it all while moving a lot.

As Sir Caveman was moving around, his heart was pumping more blood, which delivered more oxygen to his soon to be bigger brain. Dealing with the challenges of the changing environment required increased processing power. In addition to evolving a bigger brain and more brain neurons, new neural connections were being made in Sir Caveman's brain. The continuous wandering around led to strengthening of the existing and formation of new connections, as he used past experiences to respond to new situations. Sir Caveman got a lot smarter by moving and while moving. He learned to learn and he learned a lot. End of story.

Continued on next page →

Except, it's just the beginning for you. Sir Craven Caveman's story is proof that vegging out on the couch, or sitting at a desk for prolonged periods of time, is a bad way to learn. To get smarter faster, get moving and keep moving!

Exercise if you can. If you can't or hate it, get moving in other ways. If you're in a dogless house, walk your cat, who cares? Otherwise, walk the dog. Do stretches. Get a standing desk. Bike to a friend's house or school. No elevators or escalators. Climb.

The point is not to work up a sweat, but to get more oxygen to your brain. To increase your processing power. To make and strengthen more neural connections. To make learning easier and more enjoyable. To make you smarter. Most teachers won't tell you that learning while moving is the most natural way to learn. They might be afraid of losing control or simply don't know. Now you know.

The tough thing is... There are teachers who want you to stay seated for the full hour of class. That sucks! So, what are you gonna do about it?

Challenging them in front of other students, or using the tale of Sir Caveman to shine the light on the situation, is not the answer. But... Can you talk to them in private and ask if it'd be okay to stand up and stretch every now and then? Would they be willing to let you have a 3 minute water fountain break if you explained how it helps you learn? Can your parents intervene if the teacher is a stiff immovable object? The key is to have the know how and to be proactive. So for the love of learning, do something! Act.

As for the hacks I promised you... When tired, or stuck on something, or stuck and tired, stand up. Move and maybe the fresh shot of oxygen in the new blood will be the magic needed to snap out of it. It might cause a spark; a sudden flash of genius, who knows? It happens all the time! Besides, the human brain gets tired super fast and needs breaks. You'll be more productive and creative when you mix focused work with movement breaks.

Chapter Summary

Movement increases oxygen to the brain which helps you learn. How can you add more movement to life and school? Do it.

SUMMARY - Review your notes in the margins and write a summary of 3 to 5 key points you took away from the reading.

----

5 MINUTE BRAIN BREAK

KWIK BRAIN PODCAST: MY 10 FAVORITE BRAIN FOODS

Go to *bit.ly/braingrub* and and listen to the podcast. Pay attention and do the fun visualization activity which uses your body parts to remember the 10 brain foods Jim talks about. Then, recall all 10 from memory and record below.

10 Brain Foods mentioned in the podcast:

_____   _____

_____   _____

_____   _____

_____   _____

_____   _____

SUMMARY - Explain how movement and brain-healthy diet affects your brain.

_____

_____

_____

_____

_____

_____

_____

What are some active things (movement) you can add to your day to improve your brain's performance?

_____   _____

_____   _____

_____   _____

_____   _____

What are some foods you don't hate and can add more of to your diet to improve your brain's performance?

_____   _____

_____   _____

_____   _____

_____   _____

LESSON 10 - CHANGE YOUR MIND, CHANGE YOUR LEARNING (AND LIFE TOO)

BIG IDEAS

1. What are Automatic Negative Feelings (ANTs) and why do we experience them?
2. Why do you need to frame things you aren't excited about more positively?

ACTIVE READING

Read *Chapter 5: BE OPEN-MINDED* of the book *Crush School 2* below. Here's how you read actively:

1. Preview all headings, subheadings, and bold text.
2. Read the text taking notes in the margins and white spaces. Stick to 3-4 notes per page only.
3. Immediately after you finish, write a short (2-3 sentences) summary of what you learned.
4. Put your phone in airplane mode. Set a timer to 20 minutes and begin. Do not stop until finished.

What you'll learn

How open or how opposed you are to something affects how your brain deals with it. *Are there things you do to prevent your learning?*

Be Open-minded

Sounds simple enough, doesn't it? Except, students do things that prevent them from learning all the time. They sabotage it by sending conscious and unconscious messages to their brain that say *Don't learn this!*

I caught myself doing this only recently. I signed up for this summer work program for teachers with a big company to make a buck on the side. The people leading the program warned me that the learning would be intense, but the truth is that I set myself up to fail before it even started. I never gave myself a chance.

You see, summer is my writing time, but my family needed money for a down payment on a new and bigger car, so in opposition to my gut, I signed up. In the weeks leading up to the start date, I kept thinking how I would adjust to the corporate world. I even planned on writing a blog series titled *Corporate Slavery*, on the trials and tribulations I encounter during this experience.

See what I did there? I had a negative connotation for the whole thing before it even began! I also kept thinking about all the things I'm gonna hate about it and how it will take time away from writing. I wondered how the rigid, and I didn't even know if it was going to be rigid, work and schedule will kill my summer. Then I started.

During my first and only week in the program that normally lasts six weeks, I was bothered by the busy work, the 2 hour Law and Statistics lectures I was supposed to bring bag lunch to, and the unexciting lab work. I am a quick learner, but I was overwhelmed with all the new information I was learning and exhausted at the end of each day.

Continued on the next page →

But the truth is that there were 30+ other teachers in the program, most of whom I am sure were enjoying it and learning as a result. I didn't. I mean, I learned a few things, but by being close-minded I made learning a lot harder. And then I did the best thing I could have done, next to never signing up for the program. I quit!

So what's that got to do with you? Being in a class you don't like sucks. If it's not a requirement, ask for a different placement. But if you have no choice but to be there, the best course of action is to first accept it and then find things you can like about it. Maybe the teacher is okay. Maybe you get to hang out and learn with a friend. It might also be fun to get to know another student. Whatever it is, you have to start steering your mind toward a more positive place. If you don't, you won't learn.

Whether you are aware of it or not, your brain listens to all the messages you send it and is very good at ignoring things that are not important or ones that overwhelm you. It throws them out. So, even if you're trying to pay attention in a class you hate, the negative feelings toward it prevent you from remembering and understanding the material. It sucks to be in there, but if you're always negative, you won't learn much and won't be successful.

And that's just one part of it, because if you're negative, you won't be able to pay attention and fully engage in the learning to begin with. You will hold back. Something will always drag you down. And there's more…

In the previous chapter, I mentioned our really stupid tendency to expect to know something before we learn it. That holds us back too. Though it seems like a no-brainer that the whole idea of going to school is to learn, I see students beat themselves up all the time when they don't know the stuff I'm about to teach them before I teach it. I catch myself doing it as well. I bet you sometimes do it too.

Do you sometimes feel *not as smart* when learning something new around people who know more than you about it? I'm talking about situations in which you should just allow yourself to accept that you don't know it, relax, and listen with an open mind so you can learn. If you do that, you will know it soon enough. The real problem happens when you try to mask it; hide it somehow. It prevents you from engaging and asking questions. What's worse, such behavior slows down, even stops your learning.

Chapter Summary

So allow yourself not to know everything. When you do, you will learn more. You will also be more successful if you look for the positive aspects of things you generally dislike, because you want to communicate to your brain that though school and life get hard sometimes, you're ready to go *beast mode* on them.

READING SUMMARY - Write a 2-3 sentence summary using your notes in the margins.

EXAMINE AN INFOGRAPHIC

Go to *bit.ly/be_open* and examine the *Kill ANTs, Go FAR Infographic* and complete the chart below with *explanations* and *examples*. Don't copy mindlessly. Paraphrase and you will remember better.

ANTs stands for _____

Why do we experience ANTs? Be specific.

_____

_____

_____

FAR stands for _____

How do you find and accept your ANTs? _____

_____

_____

What does it mean to **Reframe**? _____

What 2-3 reframing questions could work for you? _____

_____

_____

Reframing Practice: Replace each negative statement below with a more positive one.

ANT #1: *I never do well on tests.* REFRAMED: _____

_____

ANT #1: *This essay is doing too much!* REFRAMED: _____

_____

APPLY IT

Think of 2-3 Automatic Negative Thoughts you experience the most. Write them down below.

1. _____

2. _____

3. _____

Use what you learned today to reframe the statements above. Write down the new statements below.

1. _____

2. _____

3. _____

LESSON REFLECTION

How can you use the FAR (Find, Accept, Reframe) approach in other academic subjects or areas of your life?

_____

_____

_____

_____

_____

_____

LESSON 11 - HOW MEMORY WORKS

BIG QUESTIONS

1.   How are working and long-term memories different?
2.   What can you do to move information from working to long-term memory?

WATCH THE *HOW DOES MEMORY WORK?* VIDEO

Go to ***bit.ly/memvideo*** and watch the video on how the process of memory formation happens in the brain. Then, describe the 3 processes your brain goes through to remember something. Finally, give 4 things everyone should do to boost their memory every day.

The 3 memory processes are:

1. _____, which is _____

_____

2. _____, which is _____

_____

3. _____, which is _____

_____

4 things everyone should do to boost their memory are _____

_____

EXAMINE AN INFOGRAPHIC ON MEMORY

Go to ***bit.ly/memoryhow***. Examine the infographic and write a summary of the 3 key points presented about memory.

SUMMARY - What are the 3 key points in the infographic? Explain each.

_____

_____

_____

_____

_____

_____

LESSON 12 - PICTURE IT TO REMEMBER BETTER

BIG IDEAS

1. Why is visual memory so powerful?
2. How can you use visual memory to learn vocabulary faster and remember it longer?

KWIK BRAIN PODCAST: LEARN VOCABULARY FASTER (MEMORIZE WORDS IN SECONDS)

Go to **bit.ly/vocabtip** and and listen to the podcast. Use the **Take Notes / Make Notes** strategy below as you listen to the podcast. The **left side is for paraphrasing** what you're hearing. The **right side is for making meaning** out of what you're learning.

Take Notes	Make Notes

SUMMARY:

APPLY WHAT YOU LEARNED - Check out the 3 examples below for ideas of how you can turn vocab words and their definitions into vivid visuals. Then come up with your own pictures for the next 2. Finally, use a few of the vocab words you have to learn for a class and create visuals for them. You'll be amazed how this improves your memory.

Example Word 1: Pandiculation   *Definition:* stretching oneself
Picture: reminds of the word "panda," so picture a cute panda bear yawning and raising one paw above her head and one to her side stretching

Example Word 2: Didactic   *Definition:* intended to be educational
Picture: it breaks into "did act," so imagine a very animated teacher waving his hands and using passionate speech to teach you what the word "didactic" means

Example Word 3: Xenophobia   *Definition:* fear of foreigners or strangers
Picture: Begins with "Xeno," so picture Xena the Warrior Princess running away from strange looking foreign men.

PRACTICE: Look up the definition first, then create a vivid visualization for it to remember the word and its meaning.

Word: Beleaguered   **Definition:** _____

Picture: _____

Word: Circumnavigate **Definition:** _____

Picture: _____

MAKE IT YOURS: Surely there's vocab you have to know for science, english, history, or econ. Make remembering it fun! If it's more than 5 words, do the rest in your head. If you replay the images a few times you'll remember them all.

Word: _____ **Definition:** _____

Picture: _____

Word: _____ **Definition:** _____

Picture: _____

Word: _____ **Definition:** _____

Picture: _____

Word: _____ **Definition:** _____

Picture: _____

Word: _____ **Definition:** _____

Picture: _____

REFLECTION: Explain which classes the TIP strategy will be most useful for and why. When will you use it? How?

_____

_____

_____

_____

LESSON 13 - MAKE IT EMOTIONAL (BUT DON'T BE A HOT MESS!)

BIG IDEAS

1. How do emotions affect learning?
2. Identify the emotions that help your learning and the emotions that harm it.
3. Identify ways you can use emotions to make your learning more memorable.

WHY LEARNING UNDER STRESS, FEAR OR PRESSURE DOESN'T WORK VIDEO

Go to *bit.ly/emolearn* and watch the video and answer the questions as they come up to learn about how emotions affect your ability to focus and learn.

VIDEO SUMMARY - Explain how emotions affect learning and name 3 emotions that help it and 3 that harm it.

_____

_____

_____

_____

_____

_____

_____

APPLY IT (GROUP OR SOLO) - Write down 3 ideas on how you could use emotions to do better at school. *The ideas can be about both improving your performance and decreasing emotions that harm your learning.*

_____

_____

_____

_____

_____

_____

EMOTIONS AND THE BRAIN VIDEO

Go to *bit.ly/emo_brain* and watch the video and answer the questions as they come up to learn about how emotions form in the brain.

APPLY IT (GROUP OR SOLO) - Give 3 examples of how you can control your thoughts to help your learning.

_____

_____

_____

_____

LESSON 14 - USE YOUR NOSE FOR LEARNING

BIG IDEA

1.   How can you use your sense of smell for learning?

ACTIVE READING

Read the article below actively. Here's how:

1.   Preview all headings, subheadings, and bold text.
2.   Read the text taking notes in the margins and white spaces. Stick to 3-4 notes per page only.
3.   Immediately after you finish, write a short (2-3 sentences) summary of what you learned.
4.   Put your phone in airplane mode. Set a timer to 15 minutes and begin. Do not stop until finished.

{START OF READING}

How to Use Your Nose for Learning

Imagine yourself closing your eyes, taking a whiff of the mango body mist you sprayed on your wrist, and reciting all 1337 words of the Declaration of Independence from memory. Weird? Far-fetched? Impossible? Maybe. Or maybe there is something to it...

Imagine something you're more familiar with. Close your eyes and think of "the hospital smell." What does it bring to mind? Maybe it's that one time you spent in a hospital or visited someone there. Perhaps this brings you painful memories or that cold feeling of sterility. Whatever your mind conjures, chances are you thought about something you *always* think about when your nose is treated to "the hospital smell." Why do you think that is?

Harnessing Learning with Smell

Scientists call this *Associative Learning.* We associate sensations such as scents, sounds, and tastes with objects we encounter and events we experience. For example, you might be reminded of that one pair of shoes you owned or the locker room in high school whenever you're in a crowded classroom and smell someone's stinky shoes. The more you wore those shoes or the more time you spent in the locker room smelling that smell the more vivid the memory of the smell, the shoes, or the locker room.

When we're young, we learn to associate different scents with pleasant or unpleasant things. Roses smell good. Stinky shoes do not. Typically, the smell comes first, the association later. Often, we are influenced by others' opinions of the scent. If most people think something smells gross we learn to perceive it the same way ourselves. But if what we think of a certain scent is a learned response can we use scent to learn in school? Can we use "smelly" associative learning to memorize a long document such as the Declaration of Independence?

Using Your Nose to Study Information While Awake

Scientists have asked and studied the connection between the human brain's olfactory (scent-related) system and learning with some interesting results. Studies found studying while exposed to rosemary scent improves both visual memory and our ability to memorize numbers.

Other studies have shown that peppermint enhances and arouses cognitive function and mood which improves our alertness, working memory, and long-term memory. In fact, there are numerous studies that confirm scents affect our mood. As our mood is affected, it in turn affects our motivation, performance, and productivity. And as these play a key role in learning, avoid smells you find unpleasant and give yourself a brain boost by using the smells you like while studying or working on other mental tasks.

Continued on next page →

Using Your Nose to Rehearse Information While Asleep

In a 2007 study, scientists had their subjects smelling roses and memorizing locations of various objects. First, the participants were exposed to the smell of roses and taught locations of different objects on a grid. Second, they were exposed to the smell of roses again during deep sleep. This resulted in the participants who smelled the roses waking up and remembering object locations much better than those not treated to the rose scent. The scientists concluded the rose smell cued (basically told) the brains of the participants to rehearse the information while they slept! They were rehearsing something without being aware of it! Think about how you could use this!

Interestingly, this brain cuing-rehearsal behavior happened only in deep sleep. So if you want to use it for yourself to remember facts from classes better, make sure you get enough sleep.

Why Does This (Associating Smell With Information) Work?

Knowing individuals can train their brains to remember thousands of digits of the never-ending π (pi) by using visual memory techniques, perhaps it is not so far-fetched to believe we can train the brain to use smell for recall. Perhaps you can use that mango mist to help you remember the Declaration of Independence after all.

Using multiple senses while learning creates a higher number of neural pathways in the brain. Making more associations with a concept you're learning allows your brain to build a bigger neural network around this concept. If more brain neurons participate in encoding and storing information our memory should improve. Improved memory leads to more effective learning. Thus, deliberately involving the sense of smell in learning can improve your learning.

So steep and enjoy some peppermint or rosemary tea and make sure you smell the vapors to help your brain process and store information better.

You can also use an essential oil diffuser to enhance your learning. First, use a specific scent to study specific information (perhaps the 1337 words of the Declaration of Independence?). Then, use a slow diffuser at night to make sure the scent lasts through the deep sleep stages and cues your brain to rehearse this information while you sleep.

Use other scents for other information and if you run out of scents oh well. But perhaps rethink your camomile and lavender addictions, unless you're like Joey Ramone and want to be sedated.

SUMMARY - Review your notes in the margins and write a summary of 3 to 5 key points you took away from the reading.

What are the two herbs/essential oils that research shows can help memory and learning?

Can you see yourself using either one or both? If so, how? If not, why not? _____

LESSON 15 - THE LEARNING STYLES MYTH

BIG QUESTIONS

1. Explain why believing you learn best by either seeing, hearing, or touch is harmful to learning effectively.
2. What approach helps you learn most effectively?

ACTIVE READING

Read *Chapter 3: THE LEARNING STYLES MYTH* of the book *Crush School* below. Here's how you read actively:

1. Preview all headings, subheadings, and bold text.
2. Read the text taking notes in the margins. Stick to 3-4 notes per page only.
3. Immediately after you finish, write a short (2-3 sentences) summary of what you learned.
4. Put your phone in airplane mode. Set a timer to 15 minutes and begin. Do not stop until finished.

{START OF READING} Crush School Chapter 3: The Learning Styles Myth

"I'm visual."

"I learn better by doing stuff."

Have you ever taken a test that decided you learn best in a certain style? If you have, the results told you that you learn best by seeing, hearing, reading/writing, or doing. But guess what?

IT'S A BUNCH OF DOO-DOO.

What?!?! That's right. You may prefer watching videos to reading books or hearing others talk. That's cool. All I'm saying is that you (and everybody else) learn in many different ways. Even more than those 4 mentioned above.

Believing in this poop-of-a-theory can be harmful. When you start focusing on one mode of receiving information you miss out on using all of your brain power. The brain is at its best when it gets the info in multiple ways. That's why we have ears, eyes, tongue, hands, and nerves.

Don't taste books though. That's weird. Don't be weird.

What if you tell your teachers or counselors that the learning styles theory is a myth and they don't believe you?

Don't argue with them. I don't want you to get in trouble. Just do your thing and learn in all kinds of ways. Work on processing the information in multiple ways.

Use visual learning by drawing pictures and diagrams and such. Watch videos and images online. Even better, make videos and digital graphics such as infographics and posters. Take notes, but always write explanations for concepts in your own words. Use images and text together.

Continued on next page →

Use your sense of touch by building models of concepts or interacting with artifacts related to the information. Use your hearing and listen to audiobooks or podcasts on the subject. Create your own audio. Talk about the concepts with other students.

The whole point is to make meaning out of what you're learning by doing many different things that involve many senses. In fact, olfactory aka your sense of smell is considered to be the most powerful sense in terms of making memories.

Several scientific studies confirm that the sense of smell can be used to increase your memory of concepts. By associating the concepts you're trying to remember with a certain smell you can in fact improve your recall of those concepts. This is because your brain forms more neural connections associated with that particular chunk of information stored in your long term memory. Pretty cool, but how do you use it?

Easy. Next time you have to study for a big test, use a unique essential oil or fragrance every time you sit down to study for *that particular test*. Again, do this each time you study for it, but *not when working on some other test or assignment*. Then, on the day of *that particular test*, rub some of that same oil or fragrance on your neck or shirt collar. Smelling it during the test, will help you recall the information. It sounds crazy but it works. Science says you will do better on that test.

Try it! What you got to lose? A little bit of crazy never hurt anyone. Just remember, use as many senses as possible each time you learn and study.

SUMMARY - Write a 2-3 sentence summary based on your notes in the margins and what you learned.

_____

_____

_____

_____

_____

_____

5 MINUTE BRAIN BREAK

APPLY WHAT YOU LEARNED - MAKE A VIDEO

In a group of 2-4 students write a script and record a video explaining the learning styles myth. Use visuals not just speech! Answer the following questions in your video:

1. Why does every person have his own learning style and it's not visual, kinesthetic, or auditory?
2. Why is thinking that you are visual, kinesthetic, or auditory harmful to your learning?
3. Describe how to best study information to remember and understand it.
4. Give an example of how to study for a 30-word vocabulary quiz.

Use the space below to write an outline for your video.

1.

2.

3.

4.

5.

6.

REFLECT

Write a short paragraph reflecting on what you learned today. Look at the BIG QUESTIONS at the beginning of this lesson and answer them.

LESSON 16 - THE REAL REASON WHY THEY KEEP TELLING YOU TO SLEEP MORE

BIG IDEA

1.   Explain 3 benefits of sleep and 3 ways your brain is harmed when you don't get enough sleep.

ACTIVE READING

Read *Chapter 9: Sleep Is Like Really Good* from the book *Crush School* below. Here's how you read actively:

1.   Preview all headings, subheadings, and bold text.
2.   Read the text taking notes in the margins. Stick to 3-4 notes per page only.
3.   Immediately after you finish, write a short (2-3 sentences) summary of what you learned.
4.   Put your phone in airplane mode. Set a timer to 20 minutes and begin. Do not stop until finished.

{START OF READING}

This Just In: **YOUR MIND IS A TOXIC CESSPOOL.**

There I've said it: **YOUR MIND IS TOXIC.**

Please forgive my honesty, but it's the truth. It's because you don't sleep enough.

You see, your brain uses like 20% of all your energy, which is pretty amazing considering it's not that huge compared to the rest of you. I'm not saying your butt looks big in those skinny jeans, but it's bigger than your brain and uses a lot less energy.

Because your brain uses so much energy, the brain cells produce a lot of waste products. This waste is made up of toxins that can destroy brain cells unless they are removed. The buildup of toxins makes it hard for you to focus. Because a tired brain doesn't work as well, learning is harder.

Here's what happens again:

Toxins Toxins Everywhere

Being awake produces

metabolic toxins!!!

in your brain.

These toxins impair your brain's ability to operate at its full potential. You don't learn as well, your focus suffers, and you can't create and communicate as effectively.

If you do not sleep enough, your brain cannot get rid of the toxins and, whether you realize it or not, you continue to underperform.

But there's the good news: **YOUR BRAIN IS LIKE A DISHWASHER.**

The metabolic toxins in the brain get flushed out by brain fluid when we sleep. During sleep, your brain cells rest and shrink to allow the fluid to flow in between and flush out the toxins. That can only happen when you sleep enough.

The reasons I have just given should be enough for you to want to improve your sleeping habits, but just in case let me tell you a couple more things…

Hopefully, dropping all this knowledge on you will smack some serious sense into you!

SLEEP TO BECOME AWESOMER (BETTER, STRONGER, FASTER).

Check out what happens when you get good sleep:

SLEEP ZZZZ... ⟹ **NEURONS SHRINK** ⟹ **MORE SPACE** ⟹ **FLUID WASHES AWAY TOXINS** ⟹ **YOU ARE AWESOMER!**

In case you are still not convinced that you should sleep more, check out the reasons below, and learn how you can use sleep to become better at learning.

1. Sleep = Better Memory Formation
   - Your brain organizes ideas & concepts you are learning while you sleep.
   - Your brain rehearses information as you sleep.
   - Less important info is erased.

2. Sleep = Improved Problem Solving
   - When you turn the "conscious" off, other parts of your brain "talk" and make connections between concepts you're learning.

3. Study Before Nap/Bed
   - This increases the chances of dreaming about what you are learning.
   - Dreaming about the concepts you are learning improves your ability to understand them as your brain forms stronger neural connections.

YOU LITERALLY GET SMARTER AS YOU SNOOZE!

SO HOW MUCH SLEEP DO WE NEED?

   - 5-12 year olds need 10-11 hours of sleep.
   - 12-18 year olds need 8.5-10 hours of sleep.
   - Adults need 7.5-9 hours of sleep.

Continued on next page →

I must admit, the poor sleep habit is a hard one to change. I struggle with it myself.

Just remember this:

1. A tired brain is full of toxins that mess with your ability to think clearly and be productive.
2. These toxins are also tied to dementia and Alzheimer's.
3. Number 1 and 2 above really suck.

ACTION:

If you consistently do not get enough sleep:

1. Start by going to bed 5 minutes earlier each night.
2. Decide which time you want to go to sleep and set an alarm on your phone 15 minutes prior so you can brush your teeth, text your BF/GF/BFF etc.
3. GO TO SLEEP. NOW.

SUMMARY - Explain the 3 benefits and 3 harms of getting/not getting enough sleep.

Getting Enough Sleep	Not Getting Enough Sleep
Benefit 1:	Harm 1:
Explain:	Explain:
Benefit 2:	Harm 2:
Explain:	Explain:
Benefit 3:	Harm 3:
Explain:	Explain:

5 MINUTE BRAIN BREAK

ASSESS YOUR SLEEP QUALITY - It's all about getting better at learning and improving your performance so be honest with yourself when answering the questions below. Then, decide if you want to improve your sleeping habits.

I went to sleep at _____ last night. I woke up at _____. I got _____ hours of sleep last night.

This means that _____

_____

_____

Time I get up for school is _____ . I need around _____ hours of sleep. This means I should go to sleep at _____.

This will help me _____

_____

_____

DO ELECTRONICS AND SLEEP MIX? GOOGLE IT! ACTIVITY

I keep my phone or tablet or laptop close to my bed: YES _____   NO_____

I use my phone or tablet or laptop close to my bedtime: YES _____   NO_____

Google It! - What do medical experts say about using cell phones or other electronics before bedtime? What are their recommendations regarding electronic use before going to sleep? What is the science of it? *(Use 2 or more sources.)*

_____

_____

_____

_____

_____

_____

Ask yourself: If I could, what would I change about my sleeping habits? _____

_____

What's stopping me? _____

When can I start? _____ How? _____

LESSON 17 - HOW TO RELAX & STRESS LESS

BIG QUESTION

1. How does stress impact learning and how can you beat it?

EXAMINE AN INFOGRAPHIC

Go to *bit.ly/bstress* and examine the *Beat Stress Infographic* carefully. Then fill out the chart below so you can refer to it anytime you need a reminder about why you stress and what you can do about it.

Name and describe the 4 ways stress impacts your brain.

1.	_____ _____ _____ _____
2.	_____ _____ _____ _____
3.	_____ _____ _____ _____
4.	_____ _____ _____ _____

Look at the 6 ways you can fight stress given in the infographic. Which 3-4 would work best for you?

1. _____

2. _____

3. _____

4. _____

How and when can you use them? _____

_____

HOW TO STAY CALM UNDER PRESSURE VIDEO

Go to *bit.ly/calmunderpress* and watch the *How to Stay Calm Under Pressure Video*. Then fill out the comic frames below explaining what to do to stay calm under pressure. You should include descriptions where needed, so anyone who looks at your comic can figure out the 4 things you can do to perform better under stress. Because the video shows only 3 things, you will have to **research the 4th one yourself**. Don't worry, there are many. Just ask Google.

4 THINGS ANYONE CAN DO TO STAY CALM UNDER PRESSURE

You can use any or all of these strategies when taking a test or giving a class presentation or when faced with any school or life situation that just stresses you out!

LESSON 18 - SUMMARIZE STUFF

BIG IDEAS

1. Why is processing of information shortly after you receive so important to learning?
2. What are 3 or more effective ways to summarize information?

ACTIVE READING

Read the updated *Chapter 15: ALWAYS SUMMARIZE* of the book *Crush School* below. Here's how you read actively:

1. Preview all headings, subheadings, and bold text.
2. Read the text taking notes in the margins. Include only the most important information and stick to 3 -4 notes per page only.
3. Immediately after you finish, write a short (2-3 sentences) summary of what you learned.
4. Put your phone in airplane mode. Set a timer to 20 minutes and begin. Do not stop until finished.

{START OF READING}

Even if you do nothing else do this: **SUMMARIZE**.

Don't get me wrong: **YOU SHOULD TAKE NOTES DURING LECTURES OR READING.**

But if for some reason you don't, do yourself a huge favor and find it in your heart to summarize what you can remember from the learning experience.

I know. You might have a few minutes left at the end of class and want to catch up with your peeps. But you must resist.

SIT BACK DOWN AND WRITE DOWN THE KEY POINTS YOU LEARNED.

If you don't you will not remember.

Same goes for reading an article or a book or listening to audio or watching a video. Think about it. Why does your teacher ask you to read, listen, or watch this stuff? Surely it's not for his enjoyment. He wants you to learn from it. And the best way to do that is to capture the main ideas each of those things offers on paper.

Ideally, you want to take notes, but if you are watching a video in class on the big screen there really isn't time to do that or it's hard to do because you might miss important information while trying to write down the other important points.

So... Find it in your heart to summarize whatever you just read, listened, or watched. Doing this helps your mind process the information immediately after you received it and guess what?

Learning is not about receiving. **Learning is about processing.**

Summarizing what you just read, saw, or heard is one of the best way to process it. When you process information, you greatly increase your chances of remembering and recalling it later. Additionally, your understanding of the concepts improves. In a nutshell, you will do better in school if you start summarizing most or all of your learning experiences. The trick is not to wait for your teacher to tell you, but do it on your own whenever you have the opportunity to take a few minutes to write a summary of what you are learning.

Continue reading on the next page →

So what's the best way to summarize?

The brain way, and because the brain can process only about 3 things at once focus on 3 things.

I know. Everything seemed important. Pick 3 things.

SUMMARIZING ACTION STEPS:

1. If you took notes, skim them and pick 3 key topics covered.
2. Write a sentence or two for each topic.
3. SUPER IMPORTANT: Paraphrase and Combine Information.

If you didn't take notes (and this is painful for me to accept) dig deep and write down anything you can remember that your mind registered as important.

Writing a summary down is best, but remember that you can always mentally summarize the information received. Just think about the main concepts covered and walk your mind through them. Consider what they mean and how they connect to what you learned in the past. Answer questions such as: *How are these things used?* and *Why are they important?*

This will prove huge in the future.

SUMMARY - Write a summary on what you learned. Stick to 3 key points/concepts you learned.

_____

_____

_____

_____

_____

_____

_____

Now, Haiku it. Shorten your summary to 3 lines that follow the **5-7-5 Haiku format**. This means, you have to condense what you wrote above to **5 syllables** in line 1, **7 syllables** in line 2, and **5 syllables** in line 3. Have fun!

1. _____

2. _____

3. _____

5 MINUTE BRAIN BREAK

GOOGLE IT!

Research summary strategies online and pick 3 that appeal to you. It is important to pick things you find interesting as you will be more likely to use them to help you learn in the future. If you find it lame you won't do it, right?

Source (Website name and article title) _____

_____

Strategy #1   Name _____

How to do it _____

_____

_____

Strategy #2   Name _____

How to do it _____

_____

_____

Strategy #3   Name _____

How to do it _____

_____

_____

ASSESS YOURSELF

1.   How often do you summarize what you learn?   *Always* ___   *Often* ___   *Sometimes* ___   *Never* ___

2.   What is your reason for #1? _____

3.   Do you ever summarize on your own without being told? _____

4.   Which class would writing summaries help in the most right now? _____

5.   Why? _____

6.   What is a good time during that class that you could use to write a quick summary? _____

7.   If #6 is a *no-no* when could you summarize? _____

LESSON 19 - SUMMARIZING OLYMPICS (GAMES & SUCH)

BIG IDEAS

1. How can you tell what's most important?
2. How do you get proficient at summarizing information?

PRACTICE MAKES PROGRESS

Summarizing can be difficult sometimes because it isn't always obvious which information is important and which is simply fluff that may be needed to explain the important stuff. So... How do you pick out the key points? The best way to learn how to write summaries is to write summaries because the best way to learn anything is to practice it. It's okay if at first you suck at it. It's not okay to just tell yourself you suck at it and use it as an excuse not to do it. Perfect does not exist so it's a lie to say *practice makes perfect*. It is true however, that the more you practice something the better you get at it. *Practice Makes Progress.* So forget how bad you are at it and start practicing it.

PRACTICE SUMMARIZING WITH THESE GAMES & ACTIVITIES

1) Six Word Story

How to play: *Summarize anything thrown at you in exactly 6 words.*

Variation 1: Pictures

Play: Go to **unsplash.com** and pick a picture that appeals to you. Describe as much of it in 6 words. The point is to convey so much meaning in 6 words that someone who has never seen this picture can imagine it.

Variation 2: Describe or explain something (what's your car like, why you like cats, how you solved a problem etc.)

Play: Explain what your room is like. The idea is to describe it in a way that helps another person imagine it.

2) Pechaflickr

How to play: Describe what's happening in each picture that comes up as creatively and completely as possible in a few seconds.

Play: Go to **pechaflickr.net**, type a random word in the pink box (cat, beard, pie, pants etc.), click on "Show Advanced Options," change time to between 5 and 8 seconds, and hit the blue "Play" button.

3) One-Sentence Summary

How to play: *Summarize a book you read, a story you heard, a game you saw etc. in 1 sentence.*

Play: Summarize a movie you saw recently in one sentence, so that everyone knows what it is about. Say something about the problem, the plot, the main characters, and the resolution.

Movie Title: _____

One-Sentence Summary _____

_____

More games on the next page →

4) Draw a Comic Strip

How to play: draw a short comic strip showing an event, a concept, a story etc.

Play: Draw a 4-frame comic strip showing the most significant things that happened to you today.

5) Dear Student Letter

How to play: Write a short letter to an absent student to help her catch up on the new material she missed.

Play: Pick a class you already had today and write a 1 paragraph letter explaining the main points learned today.

_____

_____

_____

_____

6) Text/Tweet/Snapchat

How to play: Use 140 or fewer characters to give the gist of an event, lesson, opinion, piece of news you saw etc.

Play: Summarize what you learned today in 140 or fewer characters. Be as descriptive and specific as possible.

Your Tweet _____

_____

6) Give One / Get One

How to play: Share one thing you learned with someone else and they share back.

Play: Describe one thing you learned today in detail to another student. He/she does the same.

LESSON 20 - UNDERSTANDING YOUR HABITS

BIG QUESTIONS

1. What are habits and why are they important?
2. What are some good learning and study habits you have and how can you maintain them?
3. What are the bad learning and study habits you have and how can you break them?

ACTIVE READING

Read *Chapter 7: Habits* from the book *Crush School*. Here's how to read actively:
1. Preview all headings, subheadings, bold text, and images.
2. Read the text taking notes in the margins. Include only the most important information and stick to 2-3 notes per page only.
3. Immediately after you finish, write a short (2-3 sentences) summary of what you learned.
4. Put your phone in airplane mode. Set a timer to 20 minutes and begin.

Reading: Habits

"It is easier to prevent bad habits than to break them." - Benjamin Franklin

Habits are things you do automatically. Many habits are good. You'd go nuts if you had to think about every little thing in your day. So, your brain does them in the background.

Brushing your teeth is a good example. At this point in your life, you don't think about it consciously. You just do it. Most of the time you don't even remember the ins and outs of tooth brushing. You know how, but don't think about it any more. You just brush and done. It's a habit.

Some habits are not so good. And, they are hard to break. Your teachers and parental units are on your case to STOP IT, whatever IT is. You try. Not happening. You tell yourself you will not procrastinate this time around. Then you do. You have the best intentions. I know. You know. But your brain doesn't care. It does it's own thing.

You have to train your brain.

This book will show you how.

TAKE A GOOD HARD LOOK AT YOUR HABITS.

❏ Poor Sleep: Do I get enough hours of sleep each night?
❏ Procrastination: Do I put off what I know I need to get done?
❏ Distractions: Do I multitask and slow myself down?
❏ Lack of Grit: Do I give up too quickly?
❏ Passive Learning: Do I expect to learn - simply 'cause I'm at my desk?
❏ Unproductive: Am I as productive as I could be in class?
❏
❏
❏
❏
❏

Continued on the next page →

For now, just read through the habits above and think about which ones affect you the most. I will talk about them all in detail and help you improve.

Are there any other habits you can add to the list? If so, add them as 7 and 8, because guess what:

I WILL TALK ABOUT THEM IN THIS BOOK.

That's right. I'm psychic.

ACTIONS:

1. Put a checkmark next to each habit listed on the previous page that you feel you could change or improve.
2. If you are ready, pick and underline the one you want to start changing RIGHT NOW.
3. Fill out the table under the **CHECK YOURSELF** section below.

READING SUMMARY - Write a 2-3 sentence summary using your notes in the margins.

_____

_____

_____

CHECK YOURSELF

Use the table below to list all of the habits that help your learning and slow your learning down.

Habits I have that help me learn better	Habits I have that prevent or slow down my learning
1. _____	1. _____
2. _____	2. _____
3. _____	3. _____
4. _____	4. _____
5. _____	5. _____
6. _____	6. _____
7. _____	7. _____

5 MINUTE BRAIN BREAK

APPLY WHAT YOU LEARNED - MAKE A VIDEO

In a group of 2-4 students write a script and record a video on habits. Answer the following questions in your video:

1. What are habits?
2. Why are old habits hard to break or change?
3. Why is it difficult to form new habits?
4. What are 3 tips you can give to help someone form positive and productive habits?

Use the space below to write an outline for your video.

1.

2.

3.

4.

5.

6.

REFLECT

Write a short paragraph reflecting on what you learned today. Look at the BIG QUESTIONS at the beginning of this lesson and answer them.

LESSON 21 - CHANGING YOUR HABITS

BIG QUESTIONS

1.   Why are old habits so hard to break and new ones so hard to form?
2.   How do you begin working on forming better habits?

WATCH THE *STRUGGLING TO BREAK A BAD HABIT?* VIDEO

Go to **bit.ly/break_habits** and watch the first 3:46 of the *Struggling to Break a Bad Habit?* video. Pay attention, take notes below, and try to remember the Tweetable Marie gives at 3:46.

Video Notes	Your Interpretation

GROUPTHINK

In a group, brainstorm a Tweet you could tweet to summarize the video. You have 140 characters. Write your Tweet below. If you can't decide on a single one, it's okay to write 2 Tweets down. Tweet one of them!

ACTIVE READING

Read *Chapter 8: Train Your Brain* from the book *Crush School*. Read actively:
1. Preview all headings, subheadings, bold text, and images.
2. Read the text taking notes in the margins. Include only the most important information and stick to 2-3 notes per page only.
3. Immediately after you finish, write a short (2-3 sentences) summary of what you learned.
4. Put your phone in airplane mode. Set a timer to 20 minutes and begin.

Reading: Train Your Brain

Your brain's #1 job is to help you survive, so it often refuses spending energy on other things. Especially things it perceives as risky.

Change can be risky. Even if the change is reasonable, your brain often sees it as risky. And, it might resist it. So, you gotta make your brain do it. Over and over.

Being afraid of change or resisting to leave our comfort zone is pretty normal. Everyone experiences these feelings at some point in their life. Such behavior can often be explained as a brain habit developed over the course of human progress. As we became more comfortable, we became more constricted.

Habits are basically connected brain neurons. The more established the habit, the stronger the connections. To drop a bad habit, you need to weaken those connections. To develop a good habit, you need to form and strengthen new ones. How?

REPLACE A BAD HABIT WITH A GOOD ONE.

Here's the "Make It Easy, Take It Easy" way:

1. **MAKE IT EASY.** It's always hardest to start something. So start slow. Say you cram before tests and would like to be more consistent. Instead of telling yourself that you'll just stop it, devote just 5 minutes to study each day. Just 5 flipping minutes! Set your phone to alert you every single day at the same time and do it.
2. **TAKE IT EASY.** Once you get going, keep going and keep adding an extra minute or two each week. Careful though! Do not try to go from 5 minutes to 30 minutes right away. Doing that might stress your brain out and you might go back to the old behavior.

When you use the "Make It Easy, Take It Easy" way to form new good habits your self-esteem will grow. This is because you will experience success in reaching goals. And it really doesn't matter how small the goals are.

GAINING MOMENTUM IS THE KEY.

You might feel that the goal is so small that it's silly...

That's awesome! It means that it will take a small effort to perform. And, you'll be able to add a few more tiny goals like this one to your daily routine.

Check this out:

Continued on the next page →

Say... your teacher assigns a chapter to read. You know you should, but it's just too much, so you don't. What if you just read one page today, one tomorrow, and one each and every day after that? It's easy! It will take only a few minutes and then you can go on with your life. In a week, you'll have 7 pages read.

Even if the chapter consisted of 10 pages, you read more than you normally would have and you are developing a good habit. That's easy, isn't it?

Forming new habits the "Make It Easy, Take It Easy" way will also build up your willpower to do the right thing. When the task or project seems huge, your brain stresses out and goes back to the old behavior, so break it up into tiny pieces.

ACTIONS:

1. Write your tiny goals out and put them somewhere you will see them often like the fridge door.
2. Put alerts in your phone that remind you to perform the action you're supposed to do.
3. Recording the tasks, however tiny they are, starts training your brain to do them and rewiring it for action.

Make it easy. Take it easy. Train your brain. You got this!

READING SUMMARY

_____

_____

_____

_____

USE IT!

They say: _Knowledge Is Power_, but that is only partially true because unless you use the knowledge you have to help you accomplish something, it is useless. Reading about changing your habits will not be helpful if you don't change at least one habit. So, apply the _Make It Easy - Take It Easy_ method to plan to break old and form new habits. Look at 2 bad habits you wrote down in the table in the previous lesson and create a simple plan to start changing them.

Habit #1 I want to change _____

I will replace it with _____

I will start small by doing _____

Habit #2 I want to change _____

I will replace it with _____

I will start small by doing _____

LESSON 22 – THE 4 R APPROACH

BIG IDEAS

1. How should your brain process what you're learning?
2. Explain each R of the 4 R Approach.
3. Explain why the 4 R Approach helps you learn faster, study smarter, and remember more.

EXAMINE THE 4 R APPROACH INFOGRAPHIC

Go to **bit.ly/4R_app** and examine the 4 R Approach Infographic and complete the chart below with *explanations* and *examples*. Don't copy mindlessly. Paraphrase and you will remember better.

1. R_____ is about _____

_____

For example _____

_____

2. R_____ is about _____

_____

For example _____

_____

3. R_____ is about _____

_____

For example _____

_____

4. R_____ is about _____

_____

For example _____

_____

APPLY THE 4 R APPROACH TO YOUR LEARNING

Pick a school subject you're currently taking and think of a big idea/concept that involves several different smaller concepts and vocabulary terms. If you want, you can even think of math or science (chemistry, physics etc.) problem solving. Then, create a plan which uses the 4 R Approach to learn this information or problem solving.

THE SUBJECT _____

THE BIG IDEA OR CONCEPT _____

USE THE 4 Rs

Receive: Were you actively engaged during the lecture or other learning activity in class? **Y | N**

If you struggled with *Receiving* what specifically can you do better next time? _____

_____

Record: Do you have notes on this? **Y | N**   If **YES**, where are they specifically? _____

If **NO**, where can you get the information? _____

When will you get the information specifically (commit to a day and time)? _____

Reflect: Did you spend time thinking about what the information means? **Y | N**

If **NO**, when will you do it (commit to a day and time)? _____

Recreate: Did you apply the information to something or make something (visual, video, used it in an essay etc.)?

If **NO**, when will you do it (commit to a day and time)? _____

What will you do/make? _____

PLAN YOUR FUTURE LEARNING APPROACH

Chances are you did not get the best results the last time you sat in class learning, but no worries. You probably were not aware of the 4 R Approach then. Now that you know, you can make a few easy changes to learn and remember more from each class. All you have to do is plan ahead and follow your plan.

Receive: What can you do better to engage more in what you're learning? _____

_____

Record: What will you do to capture the main ideas in class? _____

Reflect: What will be your reflection routine at the end of each class?
_____

Recreate: Examples of fun things you can do with the info you're learning _____

_____

LESSON 23 - FOCUS, BREAK, FOCUS, BREAK

BIG IDEAS

1. Why are both focused and diffuse brain mode important?
2. How can you hack the diffuse brain mode to learn more effectively?

ACTIVE READING

Read *Chapter 5: 2 MODES OF THINKING* from the book *Crush School* below. Here's how you read actively:

1. Preview all headings, subheadings, bold text, and images.
2. Read taking notes in the margins. Focus on the key points and stick to 2-3 notes per page only.
3. Immediately after you finish, write a short (2-3 sentence) summary of what you learned.
4. Put your phone in airplane mode. Set a timer to 15 minutes and begin.

2 Modes of Thinking

That thing between your ears is a powerful tool.

Even if you don't believe it right now:

YOUR BRAIN CAN MASTER SUPER DIFFICULT CONCEPTS.

Let me show you how. First, you need to find out about the 2 distinct thinking modes your brain operates in: focused mode and diffuse mode.

THE FOCUSED MODE

Your brain is in the Focused Mode when you are FOCUSING on the information you are learning. You might be reading, solving a problem, taking a test etc.

Why is it important?

This is the mode in which your understanding of a concept begins to form. As you recall and practice the concept in focused mode you master it.

THE DIFFUSE MODE

Your brain is in the Diffuse Mode when you are RELAXING. You might be sleeping, napping, daydreaming, playing, walking, chatting.

Why is it important?

This is the mode in which your unconscious mind is working on concepts without you knowing it. Your brain cells (neurons) are making and strengthening connections between information.

FOCUSED AND DIFFUSE MODE FACTS

1. You are either in the focused or diffuse mode of thinking, but not both at the same time.

2. The diffuse mode allows you to look at concepts from new perspectives and make connections our brain is unaware of in the focused mode.

3. To best absorb and master information YOUR MIND NEEDS TO ALTERNATE BETWEEN THE FOCUSED AND DIFFUSE MODES.

Here's the way of the warrior you can follow to learn it all:

#1
FOCUS & AVOID DISTRACTIONS when learning a concept the first time.

#2
STEP AWAY from the new info or problem. Take a break and relax. Sleep on it. Make sure you get enough sleep.

#3
Don't Give Up! Come back to it later or the next day. FOCUS again. Sooner or later IT WILL CLICK.

#4
ALTERNATE this practice of FOCUSING and RELAXING over several days/weeks.

BOTTOM LINE:

Understand How Your BRAIN Works ➜ To Understand How You THINK & LEARN ➜ To Better USE YOUR BRAIN

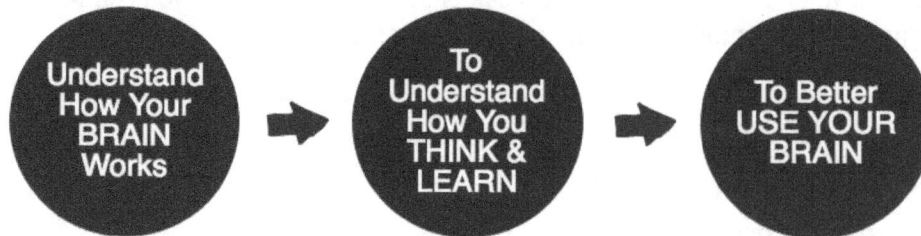

READING SUMMARY - Write a 3 sentence summary based on your understanding and your notes in the margins.

_____

_____

_____

_____

COMPARE & CONTRAST

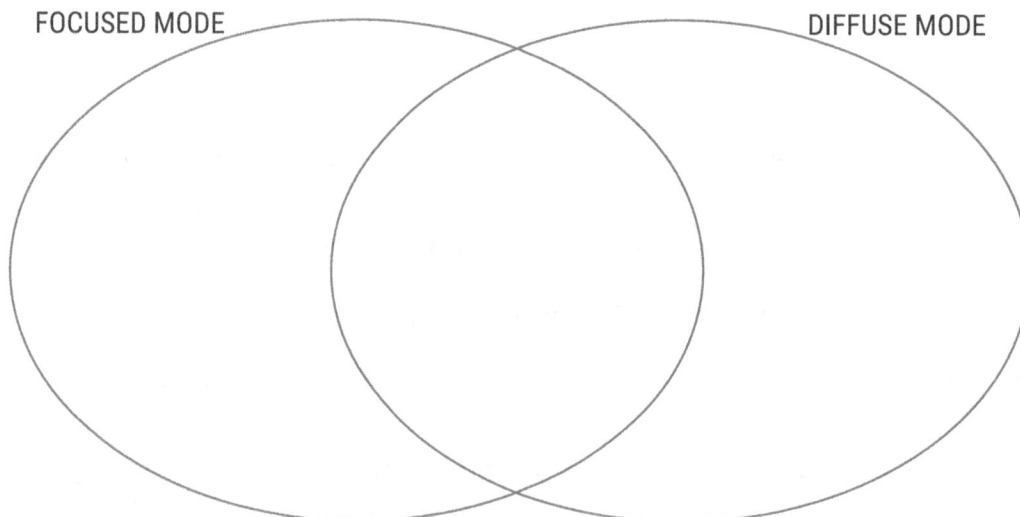

FOCUSED MODE   DIFFUSE MODE

5 MINUTE BRAIN BREAK

TAKING BREAKS MAKES YOU WORK BETTER VIDEO

Go to **bit.ly/brainbreakshelp** and watch the *Taking Breaks Makes You Work Better* Video. Answer the questions below as you watch.

Why do we become less efficient when working on something for a long time without stopping?

_____

_____

Why do our brains become less efficient without new stimuli?

_____

_____

Why do brain breaks help us be more productive?

_____

_____

_____

_____

CONNECTING INFORMATION

Explain how brain breaks allow you to take advantage of your brain's diffuse mode.

_____

_____

Thomas Edison was known to take naps in his office. He'd often doze off in his chair grasping a ring of keys in his hand. He'd be awaken by the keys hitting the floor after his hand relaxed its grip. He'd also have some of his best ideas right after the nap. Using what you learned today, write your own explanation of why Edison's best ideas came after his naps.

_____

_____

_____

GOOGLE IT!

There's a theory out there that states that some of our best ideas come to us in the shower. Research this theory online and summarize what the article or video or other media said about it.

Article/Video Title: _____

Summary:

_____

_____

_____

_____

LESSON REFLECTION

Go back and read the Big Ideas at the beginning of this lesson. Answer the 2 questions here.

_____

_____

_____

_____

_____

_____

LESSON 24 - HOW TO FOCUS (4 STRATEGIES YOU CAN USE)

BIG QUESTIONS

1. What are the 4 ways you increase and control your focus?
2. How can you use the pomodoro technique to help you focus and be productive?

LISTEN TO THE KWIK BRAIN PODCAST: FAST FOCUS AND PRODUCTIVITY WITH JULIA ROY

Go to *bit.ly/kwikfocus*. Pay attention and take notes on the 3 strategies that help you focus and get more done.

Strategy #1 is
Strategy #2 is
Strategy #3 is

Discuss your notes with your group. Fill the table above out with any missing information you get from your group.

5 MINUTE BRAIN BREAK

71

THE ULTIMATE GUIDE TO THE POMODORO TECHNIQUE VIDEO

Go to *bit.ly/pomodoroit* and watch *The Ultimate Guide to the Pomodoro Technique* video. Take notes below by writing down Steps 1 - 4 and a brief description for each step as it comes up.

STEP 1 _____

STEP 2 _____

STEP 3 _____

STEP 4 _____

APPLY IT! USE THE POMODORO FOR IMPORTANT SCHOOL WORK

Think of an assignment you have to complete that is due soon or a test you should study for. The earlier you start, the better. Set up a plan to complete the assignment or study for the test below. Be specific.

What is the project/test you need to study for? _____

What are the major chunks of information or project parts you can split it into?

_____

_____

Where exactly will you do this school work? _____

What will your work surface (desk/table etc.) look like? _____

Find an instrumental soundtrack on YouTube you like that is at least 30 minutes long. What's it called so you can find it any time?

Soundtrack Name _____

What device will you use to play the soundtrack? _____

What other (2nd) device will you use to keep time? _____

What other (3rd) device will you use to do the work with? _____

How long will each pomodoro be? _____ How long will your breaks be? _____

How many pomodoros will you do? _____

REFLECT - Look at your answers above. Can you make this work for you? What are some obstacles you might face?

_____

_____

_____

LESSON 25 - MULTITASKING VS. SINGLE TASKING

BIG QUESTION

1. How can you prevent multitasking and focus on doing one thing at a time?

ASSESS YOURSELF

What are your thoughts on multitasking? Discuss with your group and write down some thoughts you have here.

_____

_____

_____

Do you consider yourself good at multitasking? I think you're bad at it, but you might not believe me. Let's see…

Use your phone to time yourself. Start timing and write these two things on the lines below:

1. *I am a beast at multitasking*
2. *1 2 3 4 5 6 7 8 9 10 11 12 13 14 15 16 17 18 19 20 21 22 23*

1. _____

2. _____

Your time _____

Now, repeat the same thing, but this time instead of writing the full *I am a beast at multitasking* sentence and then the numbers 1 - 23, alternate between the two lines writing one letter and one number at a time like so:

I… a…

1… 2…

Start the timer and go!

1. _____

2. _____

Your time _____

Take the second time and divide it by the first time. Your result _____

This is how many times slower you were while multitasking.

DOES MULTITASKING KILL PRODUCTIVITY? VIDEO

Watch the ***Does Multitasking Kill Productivity Video*** by going to ***bit.ly/stopmultitask***. Answer the questions on the screen and take notes on the 3 tricks to stop multitasking. Pause the video when needed.

3 Tips to Help Me Stop Multitasking:

1.

2.

3.

MY PLAN TO STOP MULTITASKING

1. Use the suggestions from the video and experiences from your life to complete the table below.
2. Challenge yourself to come up with at least 3 things for each side of the table.
3. Leave room for more ideas that you get from the reading.

To prevent multitasking I need to stop doing:	To prevent multitasking, I need to start or keep doing:

ACTIVE READING

Read *Chapter 9: SINGLETASK* of the book *Crush School 2* below. Here's how you read actively:

1. Preview all headings, subheadings, and bold text.
2. Read the text taking notes in the margins. Include only the most important information and stick to 3-4 notes per page only.
3. Immediately after you finish, write a short (2-3 sentences) summary of what you learned.
4. Put your phone in airplane mode. Set a timer to 15 minutes and begin. Do not stop until finished.

READING - CRUSH SCHOOL 2: SINGLETASK

What you'll learn

You've heard why you shouldn't multitask a million times, so I'll tell you what *single tasking* is all about. I'll make it quick and give you a little hack that will make a huge difference.

Singletask

When learning something, focus on learning alone. This is hard. All the usual distractions are there. *How do you prevent them and focus on one thing only? How do you singletask?*

Enter *pomodoro*.

Huh?

The Pomodoro Hack

Pomodoro is a 25 minute chunk of time that can be used to do deep focused work. Like studying. Here's how you Get. It. Done!

1. Have a specific task in mind, or better yet, write it down.
2. Set the timer on your phone or watch to 25 minutes.
3. Kill the distractions. Phone? Airplane mode. Desk? Clear. Door? Closed. Fam and friends? Informed. You? Game.
4. Focus on and do the one task alone till the timer sounds.
5. Take a 3 to 5 minute break.
6. You can do a series of pomodoros as needed. Just remember to take breaks and restart the timer each time.

Why should I do some weirdly-named dumb thing, if I can just focus and study?, might you ask.

Continued on next page →

The answer lies in this unrecognizable thing; an edge that pomodoro gives your brain. Following the steps of setting a specific goal and a 25 minute deadline, and being deliberate about killing distractions, allows you to achieve *laser focus*. You communicate to your mind, body, and spirit that this is what you need them all to do. All your thoughts, emotions, and body parts work in unison toward the same singular purpose. This synchronicity of your whole being crushes it.

Don't believe me? Try it! I guarantee, you will get more work done in 25 minutes that you ever thought possible. More than you've ever done. But don't thank me. I'm just the messenger. You're the one in the trenches. It's all you.

You decided. You're about to crush it.

Multitasking clouds everything. Learning well impossible is. - Yoda

SUMMARY - Write a 2-3 sentence summary based on your notes in the margins.

_____

_____

_____

_____

_____

_____

REFLECT

Go back to your **PLAN TO STOP MULTITASKING** you created in the previous lesson and add any new ideas you learned from the reading. Next time you study, look at your plan and try to implement it. It will only help if you use it.

LESSON 26 - FOCUS ON THE PROCESS (AND AVOID FEELING OVERWHELMED)

BIG IDEAS

1.   In what ways is focusing on learning more beneficial to your future success than focusing on your grades?
2.   Why does chunking help focus and prevent procrastination?

TEST YOURSELF

Imagine you have a huge test in science coming up. Describe how you would study for it in detail. Be honest.

_____

_____

_____

_____

Compare what you wrote with the rest of your group. If someone shared any good ideas on how to prepare for that big test you did not think of, write them down below.

_____

_____

_____

CHUNKING - A LEARNING TECHNIQUE VIDEO

Watch the *Chunking - A Learning Technique* video by going to ***bit.ly/chunkchunk***. Answer the questions on the screen. Summarize what chunking is and how you can use it when studying for you next test below.

_____

_____

_____

_____

How much wood could woodchuck chunk if woodchuck could chunk wood? _____

TAKE A BRAIN BREAK!

ACTIVE READING

Read the passage from the book *Crush School 2* below actively:

1. Preview all headings, subheadings, and bold text.
2. Read the text taking notes in the margins. Stick to 3-4 notes per page only.
3. Immediately after you finish, write a short (2-3 sentences) summary of what you learned.
4. Put your phone in airplane mode. Set a timer to 25 minutes and begin. Do not stop until finished.

What you'll learn

Ask your future self: *Was getting that A in English more important than being able to write and communicate my ideas really well?* Ideally, both are true for you 10 years from now, but I want to show you how to focus on learning and why it leads to success that lasts.

Focus on the Process

Education is evil. Not learning; the educational system is rigged. It's set up to counteract its very purpose, because as messed up as these things are, schools often pay more attention to grades and scores than to what you actually learned. GPA, ACT and SAT, honor roll, National Honor Society; those things matter for college admission, but the rest of the world doesn't care. Not really.

The world of work that you'll enter sooner than you think, is opposite. The bosses want to know what you know and what skills you can offer. They care about the ways you fit their vision and how you can make their companies better. High school GPA? Not so much. And if you decide you want to work for yourself? I've never seen an entrepreneur claim National Honor Society membership on their resume or LinkedIn profile. Do they even need a resume?

In the meantime, parents are slapping straight A student stickers on their bumpers and no one bothers to ask what skills their kids have. That's messed up and it's a societal problem. Chances are, you've been programmed by the world you live in to focus on grades. I'm not saying they're not important, but if you stop and think hard about it... *Doesn't it seem like there's something really wrong here?!*

Okay. let me get off my soapbox before I pop a vein. Learning is more important than grades. Skills are more crucial to success than test scores. Being able to communicate, collaborate, and create in the global society is way more important than National Honor Society.

Why is it that many game changers, people who shape our world in the most profound ways, are college dropouts? Steve Jobs. Dropout. Anthony Hopkins. Oscar winning actor with ADD. Richard Branson. Dyslexic Billionaire. Bill Gates. Nerdy Dropout. Even Warren Buffett, the oracle of Omaha, a brilliant mind who invests and makes billions with scary consistency, was rejected by Harvard.

These are just a few examples of people whose encounters with formal education were less than perfect. But they have three things in common; they're rich, they love learning, and they didn't let traditional schooling interfere with their learning. In fact, they never stopped learning.

Your brain does what you tell it to do. If you focus on grades it will look for the easiest way to get grades, which often prevents learning.

So, if you've been infected with this disease, start reframing. Work on shifting your mindset from a grade focus to a learning focus. If you decide to constantly improve yourself, success will come as a result. You might not always get the best grades, but I suspect you will get good grades, and I know you will set yourself up for future successes. High school lasts 4 years. You need to think *life*.

I'm not promising you'll become a millionaire, but I know for a fact that if you don't learn, your life will suck. Luckily, it's never too late to start. It's never too late to change. I was stuck in one place, not really doing much more than my nine to five till I was 37. And then I took an online *Learning How to Learn* class and my life changed profoundly. Now, I make it a point to learn something every day.

What I'm asking of you is hard. When the amount of information you need to learn seems too much, you get overwhelmed, you start procrastinating, and you worry about grades all over again. Everyone experiences this at times. The best way to deal is to chunk.

Chunking might seem like an obvious thing to do, but it is a Jedi mind trick of sorts. When you plan things out (studying for a big test or completing a huge project) on paper and you physically separate the tasks you have to do, your brain starts to relax. Say you have 20 big concepts to learn for a final. Here's your hack:

1. Write down all the topics.
2. Group the most similar or related topics into chunks. Keep each chunk small; 3 to 4 topics is magic.
3. Write out which chunk you will study when. Be specific about the dates and times.
4. Mix it up, use spaced repetition and recall.

I guarantee the test won't feel as big after you put your plan down. Take a big breath. Now exhale. Now work your plan and crush it.

READING SUMMARY - Write a 2-3 sentence summary using your notes in the margins.

PART 1 PROJECT - ADOBE SPARK VIDEO

BIG IDEAS

1. What are the 5 strategies from Part 1 you will take with you and use while learning?
2. Why these particular strategies?
3. How do these 5 strategies work and how will they work for you?

PART 1 PROJECT - 5 LEARNING STRATEGIES ADOBE SPARK VIDEO

1. Create a free account at *spark.adobe.com* and hit the ⊕ on top and pick "Video."
2. Pick 5 learning strategies you learned in Part 1 (Lessons 1 - 26) you found most useful and will continue to use to learn more effectively and be successful in the future.

Strategy 1 _____

Strategy 2 _____

Strategy 3 _____

Strategy 4 _____

Strategy 5 _____

3. Make a Video. Title it. Organize the 5 strategies on different frames (slides).
4. Using audio not text, explain how each strategy works.
5. Give an example of how or for what someone can use each strategy.
6. Add 1-2 images for each strategy.
7. You can use *no more than 3 words* per frame.
8. SUMMARIZE at the these 3 key points at the end of your video:

1st Point: Where do you plan to use these strategies and what for?
2nd Point: Which particular 1 or 2 strategies do you find most beneficial and why?
3rd Point: How can these strategies help you beyond traditional education?

9. Submit to _____

PART 2:
GET AHEAD OF THE CURVE

What Is Part 2 About & Who Is It For?

How do you feel after completing Part 1? Do you understand your brain better and have you learned strategies to use it more effectively? More importantly, are you using these strategies? Because if you completed the lessons and you're not using them you haven't learned. If so, consider skimming through section one and reviewing the strategies that appealed to you. Reflect on them, decide how to use them, and start using them.

In case, you missed the Part 1 memo: You learn by engaging your mind and applying information and skills to creating new things. This is what Active Learning is all about. Meaning and memories are created by reflecting, writing your realizations out, discussing the information, making videos, drawing visuals on paper and in your mind, and applying the skills and information to real things that exist in your life if possible.

And now Part 2.

Lessons 27 through 45 are designed to lift you above the average. Most of the ideas contained in this section are not taught at school but help you tremendously in school. Gaining and consistently applying these skills to learn smarter and faster will get you ahead of the curve in school, work, and life. This is because you will have tools most other high school and college students don't.

That is, if you choose to learn and use them. Do it and don't forget to have some fun while at it!

LESSON 27 - HOW TO LISTEN BETTER

BIG QUESTIONS

1. What qualities make a good listener?
2. How can you become a better listener and why is it important?

ASSESS YOURSELF - Are you a good listener? What qualities make you a good listener? What should you work on? Be honest with yourself. The idea is for you to improve, not to judge so it's important you identify things to work on.

_____

_____

_____

_____

_____

QUICK COLLABORATION - Find a partner or group and come up with as many qualities of a *good listener* as you can.

_____

_____

_____

EXAMINE THE EFFECTIVE LISTENING INFOGRAPHIC

Go to ***http://bit.ly/listengood*** and examine the infographic. Then, describe the 4 steps to listening better. Paraphrase!

The 4 steps are:

H _____, which involves _____

_____

E _____, which involves_____

_____

A _____, which involves_____

_____

R _____, which involves_____

_____

APPLY IT - Everyone can become a better listener even if he or she is already pretty good at listening. Review your notes from the previous page (assess, collaboration, and infographic) and create one list that shows what you already do well and one that contains things you want to work on to improve as a listener. Remember that listening is a skill and any skill can be improved. It's important to work on it because how well you listen will determine your success in school, work, and relationships.

Good Listener Qualities I Already Have	Things I Want to Improve
1.	1.
2.	2.
3.	3.
4.	4.
5.	5.
6.	6.
7.	7.
8.	8.
9.	9.

Which 2-3 of the **Things I Want to Improve** will make the biggest difference in your learning right away?

1. _____

2. _____

3. _____

When can you start? _____

Ideal class(es) to start this in _____

LESSON 28 - RECALL / RETRIEVAL PRACTICE

BIG IDEAS

1. Explain why retrieval practice is more effective while learning than re-reading information.
2. Describe 3 - 5 retrieval practice (recall) strategies you can use to learn more effectively.

STUDY STRATEGIES: RETRIEVAL PRACTICE VIDEO

Go to *bit.ly/retrievalp* and watch the Study Strategies: Retrieval Practice video answering questions and taking notes below as you watch.

Take Notes	Make Notes

SUMMARY:

5 MINUTE BRAIN BREAK

ACTIVE READING

Read *Chapter 18: Recall & Make Learning Last* of the book *Crush School* below. Here's how you read actively:

1. Preview all headings, subheadings, and bold text.
2. Read the text taking notes in the margins. Stick to 2-3 notes per page only.
3. Immediately after you finish, write a short summary of what you learned.
4. Put your phone in airplane mode. Set a timer to 20 minutes and begin. Do not stop until finished.

{START OF READING} Crush School Chapter 18: Recall & Make Learning Last

The learning strategy I talk about here will be a game changer for you. It is called RECALL and it's been around...

Problem is, most students re-read their notes, chapters, teacher presentations etc. over and over while studying for the test.

What they should be doing is recalling.

Let me ask you something:

Have you ever studied a lot by reading your notes or textbook over and over and still managed to do badly on a test? Did that leave you wondering why?

If so, the reason has to do with how you were studying.

You were re-reading not recalling.

Don't beat yourself up if you've been re-reading a lot in the past. Many students do it, because they are not taught by their teachers the better way.

That changes right now.

SO WHAT IS RECALL AND WHY DOES IT WORK?

Thought you'd never ask!

Recall is retrieval of information from memory.

It is an active study strategy. Recall trumps re-reading (a passive way to study) because it results in deeper learning and better memory.

Research shows that recall is a more effective learning strategy than re-reading or concept-mapping.

WHY IS RECALL EFFECTIVE?

1. **SEEING IS NOT BELIEVING.** Students learn far more and on a deeper level when using recall because it involves "doing" and not just "seeing."
2. **GAINING EXPERTISE.** Retrieval from memory enhances more in-depth learning and brain chunk formation and linking.
3. **MEMORY MAKING.** Recall is a mental exercise that leads to formation of permanent memories so the learning sticks.

Continue reading on the next page →

RECALL HACKS

1. **Test Yourself:** This guards against the illusion of competence, which is you thinking you know, when you really don't.
2. **Make Mistakes:** Making mistakes while learning is good because it allows self correction and prevents test errors later.
3. **Mix It Up:** Recall in different places, environments, and situations to make information stick better.

ACTIVE NOTES ARE PERFECT FOR RECALL.

ACTIVE NOTES COMPLEMENT RECALL.

Cover the right side and only read the left side that contains trigger words, phrases, and questions.

Stretch your mind and try to remember as much as possible before you look at the right side. It's okay to peek if you gave it an honest try. Next time you will remember!

PRACTICE MAKES PERMANENT.

The more times you recall the information you're learning, the better you will understand and remember it.

Doing this will make the neural connections strong and lasting. You won't just know it for the test and quickly forget. The knowledge will stay with you!

Everyone else re-reads, because they don't know any better.

But not you.

YOU RECALL.

From now on, you stretch your brain. You make it look for and find the information that's already there.

And then you Crush School.

SUMMARY - Write a 3-4 sentence summary based on your notes in the margins and what you learned.

_____

_____

_____

_____

_____

_____

_____

LESSON 29 - MIX IT UP WHEN LEARNING

BIG QUESTIONS

1. What are 3 ways of mixing it up while learning?
2. Why is mixing it up when learning effective?

ACTIVE READING

Read *Chapter 19: MIX IT UP* of the book *Crush School* below. Here's how you read actively:

1. Preview all headings, subheadings, and bold text.
2. Read the text taking notes in the margins. Stick to 3-4 notes per page only.
3. Immediately after you finish, write a short (2-3 sentences) summary of what you learned.
4. Put your phone in airplane mode. Set a timer to 20 minutes and begin. Do not stop until finished.

{START OF READING} Crush School Chapter 19: Mix It Up

"Don't hate the player; change the game." - Steve Harvey

Changing things up when learning helps you learn better. It may be surprising, because we often rely on routines when we do certain things. But if you're studying for a test, mixing it up may be just what the doctor ordered.

WHAT you study, WHERE you study, and HOW you study helps your brain form stronger connections. When you mix it up the information is stored in different parts of your brain.

The result? You remember, understand, and use information better.

Remember Learning Styles (Chapter 3)? The more ways in which you are exposed to the information, the better you remember and understand it.

It's because your brain will store what you learn in many places. That leads to more neural connections. And connections are where it's at!

BENEFITS OF MIXING IT UP

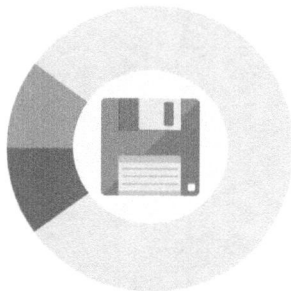

Mixing Up What, How, and Where You Study Increases

MEMORY RETENTION

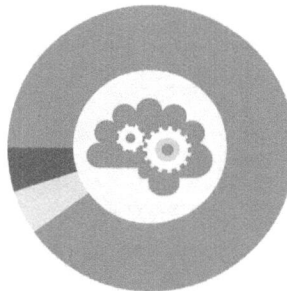

Mixing Up What, How, and Where You Study Increases

UNDERSTANDING

Mixing Up What, How, and Where You Study Increases

SCHOOL SUCCESS

1. MIX UP WHAT YOU LEARN

Jump back and forth between different concepts or problems instead of finishing one topic or one kind of a problem and moving on to the next.

Alternate more difficult problems with easier ones.

This will prevent boredom and keep your mind more alert and focused. You can also alternate between subjects when studying for finals. Just make sure you don't leave things unfinished.

2. MIX UP HOW YOU LEARN

Use many study strategies when learning. After re-reading notes, practice recalling them.

Write summaries of learning experiences such as reading, lectures, and videos. Quiz yourself on the material. Teach it to others. Form study groups.

This will store the information in different parts of your brain and form stronger neural pathways improving memory and understanding.

3. MIX UP WHERE YOU LEARN

Study in different places. If you mainly study at home, try a cafe or the library for a change.

When at home, study at your desk, on the couch, on your bed, or outside. If you lose focus, change your learning environment.

This helps you deal with unexpected circumstances. Your brain will be better prepared for any "curve balls" thrown at you. You'll be less stressed and more successful.

SUMMARY - Write a 2-3 sentence summary based on your notes in the margins and what you learned.

_____

_____

_____

_____

_____

_____

5 MINUTE BRAIN BREAK

USE IT OR LOSE IT

1. How will you mix up WHAT you learn from now on? Make a plan for 3 subjects below. Be specific.

When working on _____ (subject 1) I will mix it up by _____

_____

When working on _____ (subject 2) I will mix it up by _____

_____

When working on _____ (subject 3) I will mix it up by _____

_____

2. How will you mix up HOW you learn from now on? Describe 3 new study strategies you will use.

(1) _____

(2) _____

(3) _____

3. How will you mix up WHERE you learn from now on? What are 3 alternative places you can use to study?

(1) _____

(2) _____

(3) _____

REFLECT

Write a short paragraph reflecting on what you learned today. Look at the BIG QUESTIONS at the beginning of this lesson and answer them. If you are ready to change the way you do something, commit to it here.

_____

_____

_____

_____

LESSON 30 - SMART PRACTICE

BIG IDEAS

1. How do you learn or practice smart so that learning sticks?
2. What are some studying strategies that are ineffective so you can replace them with strategies that work?

ACTIVE READING

Read *Chapter 6: PRACTICE SMART* of the book *Crush School 2* below. Here's how you read actively:

1. Preview all headings, subheadings, and bold text.
2. Read the text taking notes in the margins. Stick to 3-4 notes per page only.
3. Immediately after you finish, write a short (2-3 sentences) summary of what you learned.
4. Put your phone in airplane mode. Set a timer to 20 minutes and begin. Do not stop until finished.

Crush School 2 Chapter 6: Practice Smart

What you'll learn

Do you read and reread your notes or textbook when studying for a test? What else are you doing? If you said many things, that's good, because the more you do, the more you learn. You gotta do different things and engage all your senses. If it ain't smart, it ain't that good.

How to Practice Smart

You're not an actor trying to memorize your lines for the school play. I love and go to school plays all the time, but learning is not an act. It's a journey, and because learning is more complicated than a play, you need to do it the smart way. The awesome thing is, that if you learn the smart way, learning itself will become much easier.

Smart practice, smart learning really, is about 3 things: *active learning, smart repetition, and mixing it up.*

Active learning is about engaging as many senses as possible and application of knowledge and skills during learning. If you've ever been told that you are a visual learner, you've been lied to. You are NOT. You DON'T learn best by hearing, or reading, or doing either. Sorry if I burst your bubble here, but I want you to crush school, so I must tell you that despite of what you might have been told in the past, you learn best by doing ALL of those things.

That's right; you learn best by using not one particular, but all of your senses. The more, the better. There are many studies that support that, but instead of boring you to death, I ask that you ask yourself this: *Have you ever met anyone whose brain is exactly the same as your brain?* Even identical twins process stuff differently.

So, if you prefer learning by watching videos, watch videos. But don't just watch videos. Read about the topic you're learning, take notes on it when you can, recall information from memory, explain it to a classmate, draw a diagram about it, or record your own video on it.

Some other things you can do with information are paraphrasing, summarizing, comparing and contrasting, writing skit scripts, making graphics, building models, and talking about what it all means. The world is your oyster. Just remember: *The more you do, the more you learn.*

Smart repetition involves recall; the constructive struggle to find the information buried in your brain, as opposed to repeating formulas and definitions mindlessly.

Continue to next page →

This is important, because as a teacher I see my students doing it wrong all the time. Many think *reviewing* is about doing something along the lines of *reading the book and reading the notes over and over until they throw up, fall asleep, or die.*

Okay, that last one is extreme, but extreme circumstances call for extreme measures. If you're at least a little guilty of doing some variant of the above, it is time to level up your learning. Do it by using *recall*.

Instead of reading and rereading, practice explaining the concepts from memory. It's okay to use the book or notes for help at first, but you want to get to the point where you can comfortably explain the concept, without any help and using your own language.

Make your mind struggle. Force it to find the information. Read over the concepts if you can't, then try it. Look at the third concept on the list and talk about it. Do it with other concepts. It will sink in. When? That depends on the amount of info and number of repetitions.

Mixing it up means alternating between learning of different concepts and skills and using different learning strategies. It works, because though you like your routines, doing things differently and giving your brain a fresh look at stuff, helps you understand and remember concepts better.

So what does that actually look like when you study?

First, don't just repeat one concept 10 times and move onto the next. Rather, practice it for a while, move on to the new concept, then another, and then come back to the original concept. If there are 5 concepts you need to study, alternate. This pattern could look something like this:

1 2 3 4 5, 1 3 5 3 4, 2 3 4 1 2, 1 2 4 5 3 etc. Get the idea?

The pattern is what you decide it to be, but make sure you jump between different concepts or problems several times, so you feel confident no matter how they're thrown your way.

Second, use many study strategies. If you're asking why, because what you do now kinda-sorta works, you probably weren't paying attention to my learning styles story earlier.

Okay, I'll spare you, but close your eyes and imagine if Sir Caveman only used sight and ignored his other senses. If he ignored hearing, do you think he'd be able to ignore the pain that follows a sabre tooth cat digging its 12 inch fangs into his back and chomping on his flesh? Fast forward to today and you're eating roadkill and dumpster diving is a highly paid profession. All because smell is overrated.

So whether you're learning in class or studying at home. Mix up the way you use the information you're learning.

Hack time. Don't blink 'cause it'll be quick. *The best way to learn something is to teach it.* The more opportunities you have to explain something to someone else, the more expert you become at it. Fact.

Chapter Summary

You can practice hard, but it won't be effective if you don't practice smart. Learn actively by engaging all your senses when studying. Use recall, which is *smart repetition*, as opposed to mindless repetition that leads to gross and/or dangerous outcomes. And don't forget to mix it up, because alternating what you're learning and using a variety of ways to learn, is where learning's at homie.

SUMMARY - Write a 2-3 sentence summary based on your notes in the margins.

_____

_____

_____

_____

_____

_____

5 MINUTE BRAIN BREAK

EXAMINE AN INFOGRAPHIC

Go to **_bit.ly/practicingsmart_**. Examine the Smart Practice Infographic and complete the chart below with _explanations_ and _examples_. Don't copy mindlessly. Paraphrase and you will remember better.

Learning Actively is about _____   An example of this is _____
Space It Out is about _____   An example of this is _____
Mix It Up is about _____   An example of this is _____

ASSESS YOURSELF - Circle each honest response

Based on what I have read today I am more of a(n)   **Active / Passive**   Learner.

Based on what I have learned today I mostly use   **Active / Passive**   Learning Strategies.

MAKE A PLAN

How can you become a more Active Learner? In the table below, list *passive* learning strategies you use and provide *active* learning strategies you can replace these passive ways with.

Passive Learning Strategies I Use	Active Learning Strategies I Can Replace Them With
1. →	
2. →	
3. →	
4. →	
5. →	
6. →	
7. →	
8. →	

What are the 2-3 new *active* learning strategies you can start using right away? List them below:

1. _____

2. _____

3. _____

Which class or classes can you use them in? _____

When will you start using them? _____

Why will you use them? _____

_____

LESSON 31 - SPACED PRACTICE

BIG IDEAS

1. Why does spaced practice work?
2. How does spaced practice take advantage of the focused and diffuse brain modes?

ACTIVE READING

Read *Chapter 6: SPACE PRACTICE OUT* of the book *Crush School 2* below. Here's how you read actively:

1. Preview all headings, subheadings, and bold text.
2. Read the text taking notes in the margins. Stick to 3-4 notes per page only.
3. Immediately after you finish, write a short (2-3 sentence) summary of what you learned.
4. Put your phone in airplane mode. Set a timer to 20 minutes and begin. Do not stop until finished.

{START OF READING} Crush School 2 Chapter 7: Space Practice Out

What you'll learn

Cramming just isn't the way to study and you need to know why so you stop doing it. Let me show you the easy brain science way to spend the same amount of time studying with much awesomer results.

Use Spaced Practice

Remember what you had for breakfast on Wednesday 2 weeks ago? If you do, you're either a genius or you need to diversify your breakfast menu. Just sayin'.

The point is that unless you remind yourself about what you had for breakfast on Wednesday 2 weeks ago every day, several times a day, you just won't remember. It's pretty useless information to begin with, and unless that day was somehow special, your brain says *meh* and throws it out.

Information needs to sit in the brain and be recalled several times for it to stick. Say you're one of those people who likes the same bowl of Cheerios or Froot Loops to start off their day with every day. I'm not judging; just pointing out that you actually do know what you had for breakfast on Wednesday 2 weeks ago, because your breakfast routine repeats a lot. You take it for granted, because it's normal, but your brain actually gets spaced practice and that's why it remembers.

Learning is the same way. Your brain stores things it is using at the moment in its working memory. If the information isn't used, your brain throws it out. This is why you, and everybody else on this planet, forget pretty much everything you learn. Bummer, I know.

So unless you meet a highly advanced alien who can teach you a way to store everything you want in your brain soon, you need to figure out how to get information to move into your long term memory.

How do you make sure stuff ends up in your long term memory? Here's a simple example. If you have a test coming up on Friday, you could study for 5 hours straight the night before. Unfortunately, much of this crammed information will not stay in your long term memory.

Continue to next page →

But, if you can find it in your heart to study for an hour each day, or can fit in ten study sessions into 5 days, say 30 minutes each morning and evening, you would have spent the same amount of time studying.

The magical thing that happens though, is that by allowing the information to sit and your brain to form and strengthen connections, the concepts are now in your long term memory.

You see, many students make the mistake of thinking that remembering and understanding is about *how much you study*. It is not. True learning, the kind that results in you being able to recall and apply the knowledge and skills you learn, is about *how much you study*, *how often you practice*, and the *time in-between the study sessions*.

But it isn't just about remembering and storing information. Spaced practice is key to understanding. For the hard stuff to sink in, the brain must alternate between the focused and the relaxed mode. It needs smart spaced out practice and frequent breaks for neural connections to become stronger and to form new neural connections that lead to the formation of meaning.

The basics of this process of meaning formation or understanding are the same for everyone. What is different is the amount of time and the number of repetitions it takes. But, as often in life, this is something you must figure out for yourself, because it is your brain and it's unique, and that's a good thing.

Hopefully, you have teachers who let you figure out concepts and practice problems in class. Hopefully, they come back to the information and have you use it multiple times over several days or weeks. But if they don't, you now know what you have to do on your own. Better yet, get a few friends together and do it as a group.

How about a vocab quiz hack that can be used for tests too? Say you have to study for a 30 term vocab quiz. Here's the hacker's way:

1. Create smaller categories by grouping most closely related words together.
2. Study 1 to 3 of those categories at a time.
3. Break to stand up, stretch etc. if you start getting tired.
4. Mix it up (next lesson) and repeat over several days.

Chapter Summary

Learning is like playing sports. If you only practice the night before, chances are you'll suck. Your team will suck too. The fans will be witness to a suckfest of a game; all because of you. But if you practice often and don't give up, you and everyone else will have a lot of fun. You won't always win, but you will feel proud and have respect, because you held your own.

SUMMARY - Write a 2-3 sentence summary based on your notes in the margins and what you learned.

5 MINUTE BRAIN BREAK

MAKE IT HAPPEN! - CREATE MY SPACED PRACTICE PLAN

1. Think of a test or a project that's coming up in the next 5 - 21 days. What is it? _____
2. Decide which days you will study/work on it and write it in the calendar below. If you can't do it every day because of commitments (work, family, sports etc.) that's okay. The point is to put down at least 3-5 sessions (25-minute pomodoros) on 3 or more different days before the project or test due date.
3. Enter 1 - 2 sessions (**1s** or **2s**) on the days you plan to work on the project/test. You can plan for several different subjects if you feel comfortable, but it may be best to just start with one and increase gradually.
4. The top row is an example.

M	T	W	Th	F	Sat	Sun
Chem Test: 1s **Eng Essay: 2s**	**Work** **Eng Essay: 1s**	**Chem Test: 1s** **Hist Quiz: 1s**	**Work** **Eng Essay: 1s**	**Chem Test: 1s** **Hist Quiz: 1s** **Eng Essay DUE**	**Chem Test: 1s** **Econ Project: 2s**	**Chem Test: 1s** **Hist Quiz: 1s** **Econ Project: 1s**
M	T	W	Th	F	Sat	Sun
M	T	W	Th	F	Sat	Sun
M	T	W	Th	F	Sat	Sun
M	T	W	Th	F	Sat	Sun

LIFE & SCHOOL SUCCESS TIP

Planning is a skill. If you can learn to plan and juggle several projects at once you will be more successful in college and in your future job or hustle. Planning prevents becoming overwhelmed and procrastination.

SO, START PLANNING TODAY. 3 easy ways to do this are:

1. Get a calendar planner and start using it.
2. Use your smartphone to keep track of due dates and plan your study/school work.
3. Use a google calendar on your laptop or tablet you carry in your backpack.

Which of the 3 ways will you use? _____. When will you start? _____

LESSON 32 - TEST YOURSELF

BIG IDEAS

1. How does writing questions and testing yourself help you learn?
2. Why is it more useful to write deep questions?

ACTIVE READING

Read the passage below actively adopted from the book **Crush School**.

1. Preview all headings, subheadings, and bold text.
2. Read the text taking notes in the margins. Stick to 3-4 notes per page only.
3. Immediately after you finish, write a short (2-3 sentences) summary of what you learned.
4. Put your phone in airplane mode. Set a timer to 20 minutes and begin. Do not stop until finished.

TEST YOURSELF

Testing yourself is one of the best study strategies you can use when preparing for quizzes and tests. It's also great presentation prep. Chances are you will be asked questions. Prepping for questions in advance will help you think on your feet and not choke when it's go time.

SO HOW DO YOU TEST YOURSELF?

Write questions about the material you're studying.

Challenge yourself while at it. It's okay to write a few "What is" questions. Just remember that asking: "What is a cat?" leads to a response that only describes what Mr. Furball is.

As you progress from grade to grade your teachers will challenge you more. They'll ask fewer "What is" questions and more questions that cause you to go deeper into the concepts. That's a good thing! It teaches you to start using what you're learning which is how you become smarter.

Let's talk chemistry. Whether you love or hate it, you'll have to study to do well in chem. Not just study though. **YOU'LL HAVE TO STUDY SMART.**

One way to do that is to ask good questions. For example, you can ask: "What is an atom?"

It's a fair question and not a horrible one. But it only tells you to look at the basics. And basics don't get no excellents. A better question, one that causes you to gain a deeper understanding is: "What role do atoms play in the Universe?" or "Compare the size of the atom and its particles to something we can actually see."

Now you have to dig deep. Find out more. Force your mind to make new connections. Really understand it. And that's how you crush it. You write DEEP questions. You answer them. This let's you test yourself, which means you're learning like a boss. You're Crushing School.

SUMMARY - Write a brief summary based on your notes in the margins and what you learned.

_____

_____

_____

_____

APPLY IT! - Read the directions and complete the activity below.

1. Review class notes you took earlier today or yesterday for a class. If you don't have any notes, look at information you're supposed to learn that was given by your teachers in the form of a handout or a book chapter or an online presentation in a recent class.
2. Write 3 -5 challenging questions (not _"What is..."_) based on this material. Make sure they ask about key ideas and not minor details, events, or dates.
3. Spend 5 minutes each day for the next 3 days revisiting and answering the questions you wrote.
4. When you review them again before the test you'll be surprised how much you remember by investing just 15 minutes in their learning.

SUBJECT _____ **TOPIC** _____

QUESTIONS TO USE ABOUT KEY CONCEPTS:

1. _____

_____

2. _____

_____

3. _____

_____

4. _____

_____

5. _____

_____

You can keep a notebook for each class and add questions as you learn new stuff. You don't have to write the answers to your questions. The idea is to get to a point at which you can just look at a question and know the answer automatically which means the information is in your long-term memory.

LESSON 33 - TEACH IT!

BIG IDEAS

1. Why is teaching one of the most effective learning strategies?
2. How can you use the "teach it" strategy both at school and home?

ACTIVE READING

Read the updated *Chapter 23: TEACH IT* from the book *Crush School*. As always: Read Actively.
1) Preview, 2) Take Notes in the Margins, and 3) Summarize.

{START OF READING}

If you can teach something you really understand it.

Think about it. Could you explain to a 5 year old what your favorite musical artist, sport, or hobby is all about?

Sure you could. You'd be able to give a lot of information with all kinds of details. It's because you studied it a lot.

I know. You might say that it did not feel like studying, but you're wrong. You were studying your favorite artist and if they are still your favorite artist you are still studying them. You see, studying isn't exclusive to school. And, it can in fact be fun.

When you listen to music or watch music videos you are learning about the artists that perform in them. What clothes do they like? What are the common themes they write lyrics about?

When you google them and read Wikipedia or other articles or social media posts they are involved in you are learning about them. What sports teams do they follow? What do they represent as people? What are their opinions on x, y, or z? Are they individuals I can aspire to be like?

So, whether you name it "studying" or not you are in fact studying these individuals because you are actively seeking out more information on them and finding out new things about them. You are becoming somewhat of an expert. All you have to do now is figure out how to transfer these learning about pop culture skills to learning stuff in school and you're golden.

I can help with that.

Let me tell you a secret about teachers.

We are sometimes put in situations in which we have to teach something we are not very comfortable teaching. We might not have taught it in a long time or never taught it. But now, for whatever reason, the principal asks us to teach it.

And we do.

And we kill it.

So how do we teach something that's pretty new to us?

Thought you'd never ask!

Continue reading on the next page →

HOW TEACHERS TEACH SOMETHING NEW

1. We read about it.
2. We watch videos on the topic.
3. We think about it and draw pictures in our heads.
4. If it involves math, we solve all types of problems to make sure we understand and can teach them.
5. We ask other teachers for explanations and ideas.
6. We create presentations on it.
7. We create assignments on it.
8. We write lesson plans (aka teacher cheat sheets), which have notes to help us remember what to do and how to do it.
9. When it's go time, we kill it!

And you can do the same. You can take notes on and summarize the texts you read or videos you watch. Then, you can describe the concepts and explain what it all means to a friend who missed class or is finding the information difficult. Draw a picture or a diagram for yourself or someone else and explain how all of its parts relate to each other. Take a math or science problem and walk yourself or a friend through it step by step.

If you get stuck on something, ask your teacher or another student to explain it and then restate what you just learned to them to get instant feedback on whether you got it or not.

When asked to create a slideshow for a class, do more than the teacher asks for by doing all of the optional parts. Before presenting, prepare for all presentations so thoroughly that you can answer all types of questions related to your topic and everyone sees you as an expert on it and respects you for it.

Prepare like a teacher does, then teach it. When you do, you kill it too.

SUMMARY - Write 3 Haikus for your summary (5-7-5) based on your notes in the margins and what you learned.

Line 1 (5 syllables) _____

Line 2 (7 syllables) _____

Line 3 (5 syllables) _____

Line 1 (5 syllables) _____

Line 2 (7 syllables) _____

Line 3 (5 syllables) _____

Line 1 (5 syllables) _____

Line 2 (7 syllables) _____

Line 3 (5 syllables) _____

5 MINUTE BRAIN BREAK

APPLY IT: LEARN SOMETHING NEW AND TEACH IT WITH AN INSTRUCTIONAL VIDEO

1. Is there something you've been wondering about recently and you want to learn more about it? If so, go online, research it, and learn something new about it. If you can't think of anything right now that's okay. Just go to *thefactsite.com* or *space-facts.com* and pick a topic that interests you and learn about it.
2. When learning about your chosen topic, do it in a way that allows you to teach it to someone else because you and a partner will have to record an instructional video explaining it to whomever watches your video.
3. Take notes and write an outline on the next page to make it all go smoothly.

Take Notes	Make Notes

SUMMARY:

VIDEO: OUTLINE OF TOPICS TO TALK ABOUT

1. _____

2. _____

3. _____

4. _____

5. _____

6. _____

7. _____

8. _____

Now practice and record it. Notice how you start remembering it all better going through this process?

LESSON 34 - HOW TO CRUSH TESTS

BIG IDEAS

1.   What are the key learning and test prep strategies you can use to do well on tests?

EXAMINE AN INFOGRAPHIC

Go to *bit.ly/crushtests* and examine the *How To Crush Tests Infographic*. Then complete the activity below.

APPLY IT!

The Crush Tests Checklist can help you perform better on tests but the key is to use it BEFORE you take the test, not after you bombed it. So, be honest with yourself. Which of the 7 Learning Activities and 5 Test Prep activities do you consistently do and what are the ones you neglect? Fill out the chart below to get a clear picture of what you do well and what you can improve.

	I always or often do:	I rarely or never do:
Learning (Class/Home)		
Test Prep		

If you do a lot of the things on the list consistently then you're probably doing well on tests. If you're unhappy with your scores, do more of the things that help you learn better on the checklist. If you're currently struggling, don't beat yourself up and start small. Pick one thing from the checklist and do it consistently. Commit to it and do it and your tests will improve. One you feel comfortable, start another.

1 thing/activity I can start doing or do more consistently is _____

_____.

Once I get good and consistent in that I can add _____

_____.

CRUSH THAT TEST CHECKLIST

You can use the checklist below in the future. It is of utmost importance to use it BEFORE the test and check "Yes" only if you did the things described always or often (as opposed to occasionally or never).

The key to crushing tests is to DO EVERYTHING IN YOUR POWER to answer "Yes" to every question.

1 LEARNING (CLASS/HOME)

YES NO

Did I make a serious effort to understand the material?
(Re-reading notes and looking at problem examples does not count!)

Did I work with classmates on problem solving?
(Looking at them doing problems does not count!)

Did I try to outline a plan for every problem solution before asking for help and working with classmates? (What steps should I take?)

Did I participate actively in group work and discussions?
(Contributing ideas, asking questions)

Did I talk with the teacher when I was having trouble with something? (Did I ask for help?

Did I understand ALL homework/classwork problem solutions when I handed them in? (Did I know where the answers came from?)

Did I ask in class for explanations of homework/classwork problem solutions that weren't clear to me?

2 TEST PREP

Did I carefully go through the study guide before the test and was I confident I could do everything on it? (Was I unsure about things?)

Did I try to outline a plan for every problem solution quickly, without spending time on the algebra and calculations?

Did I go over the study guide and problems with classmates and quiz one another?

If there was a review session before the test, did I attend it and ask questions about anything I wasn't sure about?

Did I get a reasonable night's sleep before the test? (If my answer is no, the answers to I- II may not matter.)

Use the checklist above as a reminder of how to learn and study throughout each unit of study in every class. The more "Yeses" you check, the better prepared you will be for each test. If you check 2 or more "Nos" and are unhappy with your test scores, consider making some changes in how you learn and prepare for your next test.

If you want a printable version go to *bit.ly/test_checklist* to download it and print as many copies as you need.

Credit: Adapted for K-12 from the Test Preparation Checklist for Engineering Students by Prof. Richard M. Felder of North Carolina State University- http://www4.ncsu.edu/unity/lockers/users/f/felder/public/Columns/memo.pdf

LESSON 35 - DEEPER LEARNING

BIG IDEAS

1. What is deeper learning and why is it important?
2. What are 6 strategies you can use to make your learning deeper?

EXAMINE AN INFOGRAPHIC ON DEEPER LEARNING

Go to *bit.ly/learn_deep* and examine the *Deeper Learning Infographic*. Take active notes below.

Take Notes	Make Notes

SUMMARY:

5 MINUTE BRAIN BREAK

ACTIVE READING - Preview, take notes in the margins, and summarize right after reading.

{START OF READING}

The teacher just covered a new topic in one of your classes.

What happened next?

Did you get time to practice it? Did you get homework on it? Was there a worksheet? Was there a discussion that followed the presentation? Did you have a project on the covered topic? Did you do this or that whatchamacallit?

Those questions are important. But here's one question that matters most:

Did You Learn It? I mean... REALLY LEARN IT?

Let me explain...

I recently attended an educational technology conference at which the keynote speaker claimed 80+ percent of American teachers mostly lecture. You know, we PowerPoint or Google Slide or Keynote the kids to death. Man I hope she's wrong!

I suppose lectures have their place... But what I'm getting at is that lectures have little to do with actual learning. They are meant to give information, but if you don't apply it... well... it's worthless. It's like watching a video on fixing a car. You get the info, but unless you pop the hood and get your hands dirty, you didn't learn jack. And, you'll forget everything about it other than the fact that you watched some video on fixing cars. If it featured a red Corvette you might remember that... Yep. Still worthless.

You see, I've come to the frightening conclusion that **IT MATTERS LITTLE HOW TEACHERS GIVE YOU THE INFORMATION**. Don't get me wrong here. Every teacher should make content delivery exciting. In a perfect world, this would happen in every class. After all, we are counting on the release of those really cool neurochemicals that help your brain with focus, motivation, memory formation, and all that jazz... You know... Dopamine. Acetylcholine. Norepinephrine.

But, no matter how excited you are about learning, if you do not spent a good amount of time on processing - using and applying the concepts presented - it may be all for nothing. I mean... You might regurgitate what you remember on a test, but you will likely quickly forget most of this "knowledge."

Now the frightening part... If 80+ percent of teachers mostly lecture, then how much time is given for you to process what you supposedly "learned?" Scary...

I know a recently retired social studies teacher. Dude was legendary... The legend was that if you were a student who could teach herself you might learn something. The class consisted entirely of presentations and packets. After copying the notes from slides, the students were tasked with transferring much of this information to a bunch of stapled worksheets.

Somewhere someone needs a scribe. Let's just hope the job pays well enough to cover the arthritis meds.

Continued on next page →

If you had no chance to apply what you learned in class homework is no help. If you don't know what I'm talking about talk to that kid sitting behind Johnny. He got the answers to that worksheet last night on Snapchat. He forwarded the pic to three of his buddies for a Red Bull and two Snickers bars. He's not twitching 'cause he's high or feeling guilty. He just flushed those Snickers down with the contents of a silver 20-ounce can. He's about to take flight 'cause Red Bull gives you wings.

So for the love of all that's sacred: Stop it already and go deep! You can't learn to swim by only getting your feet wet, so submerge fully. Immerse yourself completely in the learning. In some classes, you'll have to do it on your own 'cause your teachers suck. They might be nice people but they suck at teaching. Accept it and teach yourself.

Now... Let's to examine the **First Step To Deeper Learning**.

To Achieve Deeper Learning, Struggle And Make Mistakes...

The struggle is real goes the cliche. To me, the struggle is real, because it leads to ***deeper learning***, which is ***real learning*** - the only kind of learning that matters. When teachers structure classroom activities to promote wrestling with ideas, encourage making mistakes, and explain why learning this way is effective, they foster deeper learning. If they just kill you with presentations, which is called Death By PowerPoint, you must break the cycle by using more effective strategies on your own.

When applying a newly "learned" concept, ask and practice answering questions or solving problems from memory. Struggle. Don't use any aids, such as your notes, textbook, or the web. If you just don't remember, look stuff up and draw a picture or a diagram explaining the concept.

Try to sit down and recall as much as you can from the presentation, the video, or the reading you were given immediately after it's over. Write a summary or run through the key points in your head. This stimulates recall of existing neural connections in the brain, which in turn strengthens these connections and helps form long term memories. The more you dig for and recall information from memory alone, the more solid your brain connections and memories become.

Doing it this way increases your chances of understanding and remembering more later. It's okay to make mistakes, as long as you correct them later. In fact, expect you will make mistakes, as they are part of the learning process.

If you allow yourself to struggle and be wrong you will not only form stronger neural connections in your brain, but you will build resilience. As *stickwithitness* (totally a word) is a character trait of the uber successful people, it is something that will serve you well in the future.

Because the struggle is real and struggle builds strength.

SUMMARY - Write a 3-sentence summary of the reading.

LESSON 36 - HOW TO COMPLETE PROJECTS

BIG IDEAS

1.   What are the 5 things to know and do to complete projects successfully?

ACTIVE READING

Read *Chapter 10: PRIORITIZE* of the book *Crush School 2* below. Read actively (Preview, margin notes, summary).

{START OF READING} Crush School 2 Chapter 10: Prioritize

What you'll learn

Which details are the most important to understanding the big idea? What is the big idea? Can you always answer these questions when learning something new? Do you know how much time to devote to each task when working on a project? Do you plan it out? When you know how to prioritize, learning is less frustrating. It becomes easier.

Prioritize

Prioritizing is rarely taught in high school. Often, teachers expect you to have learned it in middle school, and if you don't speak up, they never find out. Then, you get lost and confused. This leads to frustration, because although you have the ability to understand what they're teaching, you lack the needed prior skills or knowledge.

For example, teachers might assume you know how to take good notes, which is mainly about picking out the important information and choosing what to write down. You might copy word for word, fearing you'll omit important information. You get all the info.

Problem with this approach is that you're not prioritizing the important stuff; the concepts that are key to understanding the main objectives of the lesson. As a result, you can't make connections between information taught now and in the past.. There seems to be no relevance either. The learning is shallow. It sucks.

How do you do it better? For one, make sure you read and write down the learning objectives each day. If your teacher skips this part, ask about what the big ideas to know from today are. When taking notes, write down the information that supports these main ideas.

Secondly, it is absolutely crucial that you know how to take good notes. Many students don't like taking notes, because they find them useless. Most of the time, the reason for this is that they write too much and don't know how to pick out the important stuff. They don't know how to prioritize.

The best way is to learn note taking in school. The Active Notes (Take Notes on the left, Make Notes on the right, and Summarize below) system show in this book is easy and does the trick But whatever note taking system you choose stick with it to develop a habit.

You should also prioritize, when completing big projects. It will help you avoid procrastination and frustration. Planning the project out in advance is the best way. Don't worry, you're about to figure it out in this lesson!

Continued on next page →

The hack is that to complete a project successfully, you need to prioritize, make a plan, and follow it.

Prioritize That Project Plan

1. **Write down the big tasks and put them in order.** If you're writing a 5 paragraph paper, this might look something like (1) Sources, (2) Outline, (3) Intro, (4) Body 1, (5) Body 2, (6) Body 3, and (7) Conclusion.

2. **Take each big task and add and order smaller tasks.** This could be (1) Research Online, (2) Go to the Library, and (3) Use the Textbook; for your sources section. You can also list the ideas to use in your Intro or each Body paragraph.

3. **Focus and do one task at a time.** Do one big task at a time e.g. once you have your Sources and Outline, you can write each paragraph of your paper based on your listed ideas.

4. **You don't have to finish in one day.** Relax, you planned it.

5. **Polish it up.** Once the project is completed, review it to make sure everything makes sense and flows. On papers, make sure you connect paragraphs using transitions.

Prioritizing helps learning and project completion, because it helps your mind focus on the most important topics or tasks. As a result, you remember and understand better and your productivity improves. Your mind holds the 1 to 3 main tasks/concepts in your working (now) memory and finds details and examples that add to their meaning as you learn, study, or work on a project.

Frustration occurs when you don't know how to prioritize info and your mind gets overwhelmed perceiving it as *too much*, when all you need is a trick or two to make it more doable.

Chapter Summary

Because your mind forgets or ignores most information it receives, you need to learn to prioritize. Learn to prioritize important info while studying and plan projects out, so you can avoid frustration that causes procrastination. When you prioritize, you remember more of the stuff you're supposed to learn. Then, you learn.

Prioritize what you do. Save you it can. - Yoda

SUMMARY

_____

_____

_____

_____

_____

_____

LESSON 37 - CREATE A PROJECT COMPLETION PLAN

BIG IDEA

1.   Create a plan of action to follow to complete big (and not so huge) projects successfully.

PROJECT COMPLETION TEMPLATE *(download more at **bit.ly/crushprojects**)*

Name of the Project _____ **Due Date** _____

1. LIST THE BIG TASKS this project involves (This should not be long - only the biggest things to break down later).

Example: *If you have to do a Science Fair Project, BIG TASKS are (1) TOPIC, (2) RESEARCH, (3) EXPERIMENTATION, (4) ANALYZING RESULTS, (5) WRITE UP, (6) POSTER/DISPLAY BOARD etc.*

1.   _____

2.   _____

3.   _____

4.   _____

5.   _____

6.   _____

7.   _____

8.   _____

9.   _____

2. BREAK IT DOWN! *(and make it easier for your brain).*

Separate each BIG TASK and break it down into a set of smaller tasks.

Example: *If you have to do a Science Fair Project, TOPIC can be broken down into (1) Research Topics Online, (2) Watch YouTube Videos (3) Find Out How Easy or Hard It Is to Get Materials, (4) Discuss Topic with Parents, Partners, and Teacher, and (5) Decide on the Topic and Begin.*

BIG TASK #1 _____

Smaller Tasks:

1.   _____

2.   _____

3.   _____

4.   _____

5.   _____

BIG TASK #2 _____

Smaller Tasks:

    1. _____

    2. _____

    3. _____

    4. _____

    5. _____

BIG TASK #3 _____

Smaller Tasks:

    1. _____

    2. _____

    3. _____

    4. _____

    5. _____

BIG TASK #4 _____

Smaller Tasks:

    1. _____

    2. _____

    3. _____

    4. _____

    5. _____

BIG TASK #5 _____

Smaller Tasks:

    1. _____

    2. _____

    3. _____

    4. _____

    5. _____

BIG TASK #6 _____

Smaller Tasks:

1. _____
2. _____
3. _____
4. _____
5. _____

BIG TASK #7 _____

Smaller Tasks:

1. _____
2. _____
3. _____
4. _____
5. _____

BIG TASK #8 _____

Smaller Tasks:

1. _____
2. _____
3. _____
4. _____
5. _____

BIG TASK #9 _____

Smaller Tasks:

1. _____
2. _____
3. _____
4. _____
5. _____

3. SCHEDULE IT!

Figure out how much time you have to work on your project. If the project is huge (like science fair), you probably have over 10 weeks to complete it so use the "weeks" calculation. If it's a paper or presentation due a week or two from now, use the "days" calculation, but use only the days you know you will have time to work on the project. But however big the project is and whenever it's due - it's best to start on it now to avoid stress later.

Number of BIG TASKS _____

Number of Days (or weeks) till Due Date (DON'T COUNT THE DUE DATE AS 1 DAY!!!) _____

Divide BIG TASKS / Days till Due = _____ ← This is the number of BIG TASKS you must complete daily or weekly.

It's best to plan using weeks, because they are relatively short. ***Write the BIG TASK "on top" of each week and then put the smaller tasks it breaks down into in the calendar day you plan to work on it.***
If you can, COMPLETE 1 BIG TASK AT A TIME. Try not to jump between big tasks. AVOID SWITCHING BETWEEN BIG TASKS, because such multitasking will be distracting and project completion more difficult.

Week 1   Dates _____   **BIG TASK** _____

M	T	W	Th	F	Sat	Sun

Week 2   Dates _____   **BIG TASK** _____

M	T	W	Th	F	Sat	Sun

Week 3   Dates _____   **BIG TASK** _____

M	T	W	Th	F	Sat	Sun

Week 4   Dates _____   **BIG TASK** _____

M	T	W	Th	F	Sat	Sun

Week 5   Dates _____   BIG TASK _____

M	T	W	Th	F	Sat	Sun

Week 6   Dates _____   BIG TASK _____

M	T	W	Th	F	Sat	Sun

Week 7   Dates _____   BIG TASK _____

M	T	W	Th	F	Sat	Sun

Week 8   Dates _____   BIG TASK _____

M	T	W	Th	F	Sat	Sun

Week 9   Dates _____   BIG TASK _____

M	T	W	Th	F	Sat	Sun

Week 10   Dates _____   BIG TASK _____

M	T	W	Th	F	Sat	Sun

LESSON 38 - HOW TO STOP PROCRASTINATING

BIG IDEAS

1. Why do we procrastinate?
2. What are the dangers of procrastination?
3. How can we prevent procrastination?

STOP PROCRASTINATING BY ELLEN DEGENERES VIDEO

Go to *bit.ly/proc_ellen* and watch Stop Procrastinating by Ellen Degeneres. Try to figure out 3 reasons we might procrastinate she talks about using life examples.

_____

EXAMINE AN INFOGRAPHIC

Go to *bit.ly/beatproc* and examine the ***Infographic on Procrastination***. Complete the chart below with *explanations* and *examples*. Don't copy mindlessly. Paraphrase and you will remember better.

1) The reasons we procrastinate are:

*   _____

*   _____

*   _____

*   _____

2) What are the dangers of procrastination?

*   _____

*   _____

*   _____

3) How can you prevent procrastination?

*   _____

*   _____

*   _____

*   _____

*   _____

5 MINUTE BRAIN BREAK

HOW TO STOP PROCRASTINATING VIDEO - Go to *bit.ly/3step_plan* and watch the *How to Stop Procrastinating* Video answering questions and taking notes below as you watch.

The 3-step Method To Stopping Procrastination

STEP 1 is _____

This means _____

_____

STEP 2 is _____

This means _____

_____

STEP 3 is _____

This means _____

_____

APPLY IT - MAKE A PLAN FOR YOUR NEXT PROJECT

Project to Complete (Study for Math Test, English Essay, History Presentation etc.) _____

STEP 1 - Organize it into bite-sized chunks

TASK TO DO	WHAT DAY & HOW MUCH TIME

STEP 2 - What are 1-2 fun tasks you can start the project with? _____

_____

STEP 3 - What are possible distractions I need to avoid? _____

_____

LESSON 39 - THE REAL DEAL ON CRAMMING & HACKING CRAMMING

BIG IDEAS

1. Why is cramming ineffective?
2. Explain the Primacy Effect and Recency Effect and how to use them to hack cramming.

THE SCIENCE BEHIND MEMORY VIDEO

Go to **bit.ly/nocramming** and watch *The Science Behind Memory Video* answering questions on the screen.

VIDEO SUMMARY - Summarize the 3 key points discussed in the video.

_____

_____

_____

ACTIVE READING: WHAT'S THE BRAIN DEAL WITH CRAMMING?

Preview before reading, take notes in the margins as you read, and summarize right after you read.

{START OF READING}

Cramming. The answer to studying for many students.

I get it. We all have a life and school often ain't it until we have no choice.

No one plans to cram. It's not like you say to yourself: *I will study for my chemistry test from midnight to 4 am the night before and sleep for 3 hours that night.* That's cray-cray! Who in their right mind would plan to study for 4 hours straight and sleep for 3 hours? Yet, many students wait till the night before to hit the books or review for that big history, science, or english test. They promise themselves to not procrastinate, but end up waiting till the very last moment to write that essay or create that presentation. Is this you?

But Is Cramming Effective?

One time, a female student came to see me after school. She bombed her chem test and was bummed out about it. *I studied for four hours last night and I thought I knew it! I even stayed up late to go over everything twice! I don't understand how I did so bad! Is there any extra credit I can do?*

True story except it's kind of a lie. This wasn't just one student. I hear this all the time from many students. The truth might be that many just don't know why cramming is ineffective. I mean you might go to sleep feeling you've got it. And then the test comes and you don't... Why is that?

Well... What happened was...

The information never made it from short term to long term memory.

Continue to next page →

In other words: *You never actually learned it.* Your brain threw it out. The hippocampus, which is the part of the brain that holds short term memories and decides whether to keep them or not, decided much of the information wasn't important enough to keep and so it hit the *DELETE* button. You might have even understood it, but you still forgot it. And you can't use that which you don't remember. Bummer, I know.

Cramming sucks, because you spend a lot of time doing it while results you get are mediocre at best. Even if you do well on the test you crammed for you forget the information shortly after you take the test. That's not too terrible if you don't need it anymore. But what if the same stuff reappears on the final, or you need to use it on a project, or in your future job?

The real tragedy happens when you realize that though you did okay on the test you crammed for you did not learn anything. Not really. If you forgot it all a day or two later, you're not any smarter and you just wasted a bunch of time going to school and cramming. Your brain might have held the information until the morning of the test, but then closed the loop on it and threw it out after you completed the test.

But most likely, the lack of sleep and not enough time for the information to be processed affected your performance negatively. You probably did not do as well as you could have had you used smart spaced practice. Hopefully, you weren't one of those school zombies who chronically don't get enough sleep and look like they have more than a few dead brain cells up there.

So What's The Real Deal On Cramming?

Why does it seem like cramming can sometimes work?

As I mentioned above, your brain, specifically the hippocampus is capable of holding a bunch of information for immediate use. What does *immediate* mean in this context? It's hard to say, but the time span is short. It may be 2 hours or 2 days, but probably not 2 weeks. And, unless you are revisiting the information periodically, your memories of it fade away more and more with each passing hour.

Some people are better at holding information than others. One reason for this may be genetic, another is most likely a measure of how well-trained your brain is at cramming. What this means is that you might temporarily remember more facts than someone else and hold them in your working memory longer.

So... You might do well on a test, but the information often doesn't make it to long term memory. It is temporarily stored a bit longer. You might remember more facts for a test you crammed for than the next person, but will still forget most of the information in the long term. In a nutshell, you did well on the test, but still didn't learn the concepts because your hippocampus threw them out after you used them for the test.

The way you study communicates to your unconscious brain if the information will be needed in the future. This is why the depth of your learning depends on your approach to learning. Consequently, deeper learning cannot occur when you cram.

This might be okay for subjects and concepts you'll never use in the future. If you just want to get through... say physics, and you don't care about getting an A or a B, cramming tactics might help with that... But why would anyone cram for something they really want to learn? Personally, I don't think anyone wishes to do that with topics they're passionate about, but most students fail to plan their study sessions out. This is why you end up cramming. **You don't plan not to cram.**

Why LeBron Doesn't Cram

If you want to be successful in your future profession, you will have to become smarter than most people in your field, which means that you need to approach studying it for the long term. The use it and then lose it way that cramming is does not allow you to be in the top 10% of your field of work. Would we be calling LeBron James "The King" or "King James" now had he just took a thousand shots on the night before the game and skipped practice all the other days? **Much like LeBron has to practice repeatedly to maintain his high level of play you need to use strategies that help you retain information.**

Continue to next page →

How do you do that? LeBron has coaches who help him with workout regimens and conditioning. These coaches also schedule team practices. Most of these things are routines; non-negotiables he might not like as much as playing basketball, but has to do to stay successful. So what are your non-negotiables? What are the subjects you must not neglect and cram for? Decide and create a plan of practice that will get you to the top.

The Future Does Not Favor Those Who Cram

But here's the deal. You never know when a subject you decided to ignore and only study for last minute might become useful. Maybe 10 years from now, you're a businessman who scored a big account, an engineering firm that builds roads, bridges, and skyscrapers, and it quickly becomes apparent to you that you need basic physics knowledge to be able to understand your new client's needs and what the people you are meeting with are talking about.

You want to hit a homerun with this one, and maybe you can even do a half-decent job, but your boss quickly finds out that Jennifer who just got hired can do a lot better job, because she took high school science seriously and just proposed an excellent idea for how to solve the new client's problem. This is something you couldn't do in the moment and had no time to learn in the present. Jennifer is the new account manager and you hope to be ready the next time an opportunity like this one comes along…

Luckily, that didn't happen yet. Your future is all ahead of you. Jennifer is a 9th grader killing it in biology and thinking she might become a lawyer like her aunt Penelope or an entrepreneur like her dad. You are in physics, because your college of choice requires it for admission and you're getting by. You have a respectable B average, but forgot most of what you were supposed to learn last month, because you already took that test. You can say: *Who cares? It's not like some freshman will outperform me in the future.* Or, you can **think long term and always seek to get something out of every class you take**.

The truth is that in the present you just don't know how or when understanding ideas outside of your expertise may help your future success. You might not always have a choice which classes to take, but you can always decide if you spend your time blowing them off or crushing them. Make the choice that will feel good 5, 10, and 50 years from now.

5 MINUTE BRAIN BREAK

EXAMINE AN INFOGRAPHIC: HACKING CRAMMING

Go to *bit.ly/hackcramming*. Examine the **Hacking Cramming Infographic** and explain the 4 ways to improve your cram sessions. Use *examples*. Don't copy mindlessly. Paraphrase and you will remember better.

Cramming Strategy #1 is _____ Why use it? _____

_____

For example _____

Cramming Strategy #2 is _____ Why use it? _____

_____

For example _____

Cramming Strategy #3 is _____ Why use it? _____

_____

For example _____

Cramming Strategy #4 is _____ Why use it? _____

_____

For example _____

APPLY IT

1. Imagine you have a vocab quiz tomorrow and you forgot about it until now. You friend just texted you asking how studying is going and it's 10 pm. What do you do?
2. Use the list of words below (or vocab from your actual class) to show how you can apply the 4 cramming hacks you learned to studying for this quiz in the next 2 hours.
3. Brainstorm, write a script, and record a video explaining your 2-hour Cram Plan. Use visual examples.

Vocab: 1) Atom, 2) Element, 3) Compound, 4) Mixture, 5) Isotope, 6) Ion, 7) Cation, 8) Anion, 9) Covalent Bonding, 10) Ionic Bonding, 11) Molecule, 12) Formula Unit, 13) Polyatomic Ion, 14) Alloy, 15) Metallic Bonding.

Script/Outline:

1. _____

2. _____

3. _____

4. _____

5. _____

6. _____

7. _____

Visuals:

LESSON 40 - HACKING CRAMMING WITH SPACED PRACTICE

BIG IDEAS

1. How can you use spaced practice when cramming?

WATCH A VIDEO: BART PROCRASTINATES…

Go to **bit.ly/bartcrams** and watch the video.

Martin to Bart: *A blindfolded chimp with a pencil in his teeth has a better chance of passing this test than you do.*

VIDEO SUMMARY - Brainstorm and summarize the key points of the video with a similar sarcastic quote.

_____

_____

ACTIVE READING:

1. Read the excerpt below from *Chapter 18: Space It Out* from the book *Crush School*.
2. Preview before reading, take notes in the margins as you read, and summarize right after you read.

{START OF READING}

HACKING PROCRASTINATION

Twas the night before Test Day, when all through the house
Not a creature was stirring, not even a mouse.
The pages were spread on your desk with care,
In hopes that all knowledge would enter from there.

The others were nestled all snug in their beds,
While visions of Aced tests danced in their heads.
But your books, and your notes, and you thinking "Man!,"
Had just settled your brains for a last minute cram…

I am *not* advocating for the Last Resort Tactic I'm about to give you!

Do everything in your power to space your learning out over several days, or weeks if possible, because that's how you get your brain to remember and understand best.

But, if against my best advice, you ended up putting your studies off until the last possible moment, use the Crush School Last Resort Cram Tactic.

Continue to next page →

CRUSH SCHOOL LAST RESORT CRAM TACTIC

1.   Are you planning to study for 4 hours the night before a test? Don't.
2.   Instead, study for 2 hours, go to sleep, and wake up 2 hours earlier the next day to study for 2 more hours.

Seems like it's all the same right?

Wrong!

Sure, you get the same amount of sleep and study time. But, by "sleeping on it" you're allowing time for your brain to process and link information. This makes stronger neural connections.

Studying after you sleep gives you a fresh look at the concepts and makes these neural connections even stronger!

The catch is that **If You Don't Sleep, None Of It May Matter**.

SUMMARY: Summarize the reading above in exactly 1 sentence. Include only the most important point.

_____

_____

5 MINUTE BRAIN BREAK

APPLY IT!

1.   Modify your plan from yesterday to include last minute spaced practice described above.
2.   Record a new video that includes what you talked about yesterday and what you learned today.

Video Outline:

1.   _____

2.   _____

3.   _____

4.   _____

5.   _____

6.   _____

7.   _____

LESSON 41 - HOW TO BECOME MORE OPEN-MINDED

BIG QUESTIONS

1. Why is it natural to resist change even though it's often beneficial to try new things?
2. Explain the 3 steps you can take to become more open-minded to new and different ideas.

EXAMINE THE MORE OPEN-MINDED IN 3 STEPS INFOGRAPHIC

Go to **bit.ly/op_mind** and examine the infographic. Then, describe the 3 steps to becoming more open-minded.

The 3 steps are:

1. _____, which is _____

_____

2. _____, which is _____

_____

3. _____, which is _____

_____

What are the benefits of becoming more open-minded?

_____

_____

_____

_____

LESSON REFLECTION - No one is completely open-minded or narrow-minded. Everyone is more open-minded about some things and less about others. What are some areas of school/life you consider yourself more open-minded about? What are some school things (classes, habits, behaviors etc.) you could become more open-minded about? How would this help you do better in school?

_____

_____

_____

_____

_____

LESSON 42 - TEAMWORK BASICS

BIG IDEAS

1. What does it take to be an effective team member?
2. How might your ability to work on a team affect your future?

TEAM COMPETITION

In teams of 3 to 4 construct a bridge spanning a 40 cm gap between 2 chairs that can hold a 0.5 liter bottle of water.

1. You can use only 10 pieces of newspaper.
2. No tape, glue, or any other materials than the newspaper itself.
3. You can cut, rip, deform the newspaper in any way you decide.
4. You have 10 minutes.
5. Use the space below for ideas, notes, and designs.

TEST YOUR BRIDGE

How did you do? _____

What were some reasons for your failure/success? _____

_____

_____

WATCH A VIDEO ABOUT BUILDING A TEAM

Go to *bit.ly/teampersonas* and take notes below whenever the video pauses.

Explain who the **Performer** on any team is _____

_____

Explain who the **Highly Effective Doer** is _____

_____

How is the **Less Effective Doer** different? _____

_____

What does **PTS** stand for? Who is he? _____

_____

What does **SP** stand for? Who is he? _____

_____

REFLECT

Think back to the bridge competition earlier. What could you have done differently?

_____

_____

_____

Which one of the 5 team personas shown in the video were you during the project?

_____

Back your answer above with 2-3 examples of how you contributed to the team.

_____

_____

Which of the 5 personas does your work ethic represent the most when working on group projects in school?

_____

How might this matter in your future? _____

_____

LESSON 43 - MAKE TEAMWORK WORK FOR YOU

BIG IDEAS

1. What are the ingredients of effective teamwork?
2. What should your teamwork participation look like so you learn?

WATCH THE *GROUP ASSIGNMENTS* VIDEO

Go to ***bit.ly/group_work*** and watch the first 4:00 of the *Group Assignments* video.

QUICK WRITE - React to the video. Include past experiences, examples, and how you felt.

_____

_____

_____

_____

ACTIVE READING:
1. Read *Chapter 21: Team Up* from the book *Crush School* below.
2. Preview, take notes in the margins, and summarize right after reading.

{START OF READING}

"The first principle is that you must not fool yourself and you are the easiest person to fool."   - Richard Feynman

Why is it a good idea to work in a group?

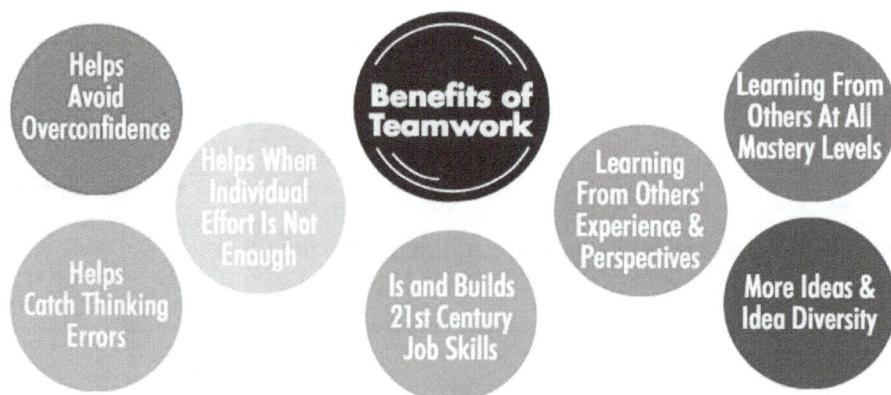

Helps Avoid Overconfidence

Helps When Individual Effort Is Not Enough

Helps Catch Thinking Errors

Benefits of Teamwork

Is and Builds 21st Century Job Skills

Learning From Others' Experience & Perspectives

Learning From Others At All Mastery Levels

More Ideas & Idea Diversity

Bottom Line: Whether you like it or not you will have to work well with people in the future.

Even if you become the boss you'll have to collaborate, rather than boss others around.

Doing it the old school way gets you the middle finger and a "see ya!" in the world of today.

Continued on next page →

Resisting teamwork is normal. It's because our brain focuses on survival and automatically fears trusting others. But you must remember that this is the new age and the likelihood of getting our skull cracked with a club is very low.

Besides, we have a tendency to "fill in the blanks" or create "understandings" that are false when we don't know or fear something. Collaboration helps you avoid such nonsense.

STUDY GROUPS

It's always a good idea to get a study group going on your own. It's an awesome way to be proactive.

This is how you become a better leader. You organize when, where, and how. You get others on board. You keep yourself and others committed. You study, teach, and learn from each other.

Keep your study group small. 3 to 4 people is ideal. Pick people who can focus and help you learn. Be honest with yourself. Will you be productive if you work with your best friend? Yes? Maybe? Not really?

You can meet before or after school in the school library, or Starbucks, or somebody's house.

Chances are that if you organize it in your house, your mom will get you snacks or bake a cake - she'll be so proud of you taking control of your learning. And she'll want to support you 100%.

It will score you some serious points with dad too, which will come in handy when it's time to ask for those car keys or a different perk.

But don't tell them I told you. Just let it happen.

When forming a study group it's important to understand that effective teamwork doesn't just happen.

Good teamwork habits have to be formed and developed so that group goals are accomplished and everyone in the group benefits from participation in it.

And the best way to get good at collaboration is to do it.

Check this out.

There are times when I see a student contribute little to the group. For example, the "group manager" might skip out on intellectual work.

That's a real bummer, because this is where all of the action happens!

Continued on next page →

Being involved in the brainstorming and decision making is how you best learn content and collaboration.

So don't be "just" the "manager." Become a mastermind.

CRUSH SCHOOL MASTERMINDS

The #1 purpose of a Mastermind group is to help all group members achieve success.

Here's how:

1.   You have clear goals and agenda when you meet.
2.   You brainstorm and learn together.
3.   You are honest, respectful, and compassionate.
4.   You hold yourself and everyone else accountable.
5.   You support one another.

Check out the 4 necessary ingredients to building an effective team on the next page.

BUILDING AN EFFECTIVE MASTERMIND GROUP

1. TEAM CULTURE

- "In This Together"

- Common Goals

2. SAFETY, SUPPORT, GROWTH

- Mutual Respect

- Openness (No Idea Is Dumb)

- Taking Risks Encouraged

- Feedback, Not Criticizing

3. HIGH EXPECTATIONS

- Set Rules & Norms

- Everyone Contributes

- Everyone Is Accountable

4. TIME

- It Takes Time To Click

- Hiccups Happen

- Keep Team Together

- Be Consistent

SUMMARY - Write a summary of the reading using your notes and interpretations.

_____

_____

_____

_____

_____

_____

5 MINUTE BRAIN BREAK

SMALL GROUP PROJECT: Make a Paper Slide Video in a Group of 2 or 3.

Directions:
1. Make a paper slide video (Go here to see what it should look like → ***http://bit.ly/paperslidevid***).
2. Research an active learning strategy from the following **LIST OF TOPICS:**

    - Previewing & Summarizing
    - Active Note Taking
    - Active Reading
    - Teaching Concepts to Others
    - Drawing Pictures and Diagrams / Making Models
    - Recall / Retrieval Practice
    - Organization / Pattern Recognition
    - Creating Memory Palaces for Learning Vocab
    - Multiple Approaches To Learning
    - Collaborative Work / Study Groups
    - Interleaving (Mixing it up)
    - Testing Yourself
    - Reorganizing Information
    - Making/Correcting Your Own Mistakes
    - Relating New Information To What You Know

3. **Questions to answer** in your Paper Slide Video:
    - Describe the learning strategy in detail.
    - Give an example of how someone would do it.
    - Explain why it is considered an active (not passive) learning strategy.
    - Why does it work?
    - What is the science behind it (what happens in the brain?)?
    - Give another example of how someone can do it.
    - Summarize the strategy in 3 key points.
4. Upload to YouTube and share the link with your teacher in a Padlet or Google Docs.

LESSON 44 - TO SUCCEED, FAIL OFTEN

BIG IDEAS

1. Why is failure necessary to success?
2. What are some ways you can make failure less of a big deal?

ACTIVE READING:

1. Read *Chapter 20: Failure Is The Only Option* from the book *Crush School* below.
2. Preview, take notes in the margins, and summarize right after reading.

{START OF READING}

"Stay hungry. Stay foolish." - Steve Jobs

Failure is the only option?

What?!?!

Isn't this book supposed to help you crush school, not fail it?

Yes it is. Chill. The failure I'm talking about is of the good variety, because it helps you succeed.

Take Steve Jobs. He was a pretty successful and brilliant dude. Where would we be without iTunes, smartphones, and tablets? Steve's success though was mainly a result of his attitude toward failure. While brilliant, he failed at Apple the first time around and resigned in 1985. He came back again in 1997 and lead the company out of bankruptcy to the awesomeness that it is today.

Oh, and after first leaving Apple, he founded Pixar and revolutionized movie animation, because he could. He then came back to Apple and crushed it.

How did Steve do it?

1. He failed a lot.
2. Instead of crying about it, he learned from his failures.

The path to greatness is filled with failure and only those who take risks, fail, and learn from their mistakes achieve it.

Truth Bomb: Many students are afraid to make mistakes, so they don't take enough risks in school.

As a result, they never learn to fail forward.

Continued on next page →

FAILING FORWARD

"I can accept failure, everyone fails at something. But I can't accept not trying."

- Michael Jordan aka the G.O.A.T.

Failing forward is understanding that **FAILING DOES NOT MAKE YOU A FAILURE.**

If you see yourself as a failure, you will be a failure. This is because you are training your brain to accept you as a failure. And failure behaviors follow.

To be successful, you need to change how you view failure. So, read, accept, believe, and live these truths:

1. **Failure is tough. It's also unavoidable. I accept it will happen to me and I plan to learn from it.**
2. **Failure is temporary, so I will take risks.**
3. **Everyone fails, but successful people like me view failure as the beginning, not the end.**
4. **The more I fail, the more I succeed.**

Check out the example below to learn how the right approach to failure can help you become a better learner.

RANDOM DAY IN CLASS: Teacher asks a question.

OPTION 1: You don't answer. You think you may know it, but don't want to be wrong. You often forget the answer the teacher gave to her own question.

OPTION 2: You answer. You get it wrong. The teacher corrects you. You remember it and you answer 5 questions related to it right on the test.

ANALYSIS: It doesn't take a genius to figure out that OPTION 2 is better. But why?

Mostly, it has to do with the fact that when you fail to answer correctly, your mind remembers the answer given as a correction. Also, you might have felt a little embarrassed speaking up and being wrong. Your brain remembers the feeling associated with this event and makes more neural connections. Thus, you remember and learn better.

FINAL THOUGHTS ON FAILURE

Whether in class or studying at home, never tell yourself "I Don't Know."

At the very least, attempt to answer the question, define the word, or explain the concept. If you're really struggling, say something connected to it. Be wrong now, so you can be right later. Fail forward.

Truth Bomb: When you say "I Don't Know" you tell your brain "Don't Learn This."

I'm not ready to accept that. Are you?

REFLECTION: What are your thoughts on failure? Why do people fear it? How can you overcome fearing failure? How can taking risks and failing help your success?

Would you be open-minded about stepping out of your comfort zone and taking a risk at school? Do you sometimes know the answer but never answer? Do you always work alone? Do you always play it safe? What is something you could try today that will feel awkward or make you nervous that you know can make a difference in your learning?

Write it down below. Describe what the deal is.

If you're not ready to do it all at once, what is a small thing you can do today to start overcoming it?

What could the next small step look like?

And the next?

What will the benefits to you be if you can overcome it?

LESSON 45 - STAY CURIOUS GRASSHOPPER

BIG IDEAS

1. Compare and contrast Diversive and Epistemic Curiosity.
2. Why does curiosity decline as you get older and how can you reawaken it?
3. What are the benefits of always working to remain curious?

EXAMINE AN INFOGRAPHIC

Go to *bit.ly/remaincurious* and examine the CURIOSITY INFOGRAPHIC. Take active notes below. Paraphrase.

Take Notes	Make Notes

SUMMARY:

REFLECT - Be honest with yourself as this exercise is meant to help you identify things that can help you become more successful by staying *curious*. To do this, you need to reflect on things that cause you to be *incurious* at times.

Describe your use of digital devices. Talk about what devices you use, how often, and how many hours per day.

Epistemic Curiosity is intentional and helps you learn. *Diversive* Curiosity is often impulsive and superficial. For example, when you go on YouTube to figure out how to use mascara your curiosity can be described as epistemic, but when you watch video after video of outrageous makeups diversive curiosity has you in it's grip and you're wasting time. Curiosity is all about having a balance: of course you want to have fun but you have to be careful not to get sucked down a rabbit hole that has you wasting an hour or two learning absolutely nothing.

What are the activities **you do** that stimulate your Epistemic curiosity?

How often is your device time Epistemic?

What are the activities **you do** that use your Diversive curiosity?

How often is your device time Diversive?

Overall, is your device time more Epistemic or Diversive? Explain.

What should you change? What should you keep?

PART 2 PROJECT - ADOBE SPARK WEB PAGE

BIG IDEAS

1. What are the 5 strategies from Part 2 you will take with you and use while learning?
2. Why these particular strategies?
3. How do these 5 strategies work and how will they work for you?

SPART 2 PROJECT - 5 LEARNING STRATEGIES ADOBE SPARK WEB PAGE

1. Create a free account at **spark.adobe.com** and hit the ⊕ on top and pick "Page."
2. Pick 5 learning strategies you learned in Part 2 (Lessons 27 - 45) you found most useful and will continue to use to learn more effectively and be successful in the future.

Strategy 1 _____

Strategy 2 _____

Strategy 3 _____

Strategy 4 _____

Strategy 5 _____

3. Make a Web Page. Title it. Organize the 5 strategies in the space provided.
4. In one sentence, explain how each strategy works.
5. Give an example of how or for what someone can use each strategy.
6. Add 1-2 images for each strategy.
7. Put a SUMMARY at the bottom that explains these 3 key points:

1st Point: Where do you plan to use these strategies and what for?
2nd Point: Which particular 1 or 2 strategies do you find most beneficial and why?
3rd Point: How can these strategies help you beyond traditional education?

8. Submit to _____

PART 3:
Accelerate And Don't Look Back

WHAT IS PART 3 ABOUT & WHO IS IT FOR?

So, you've build a platform and replaced the learning strategies that didn't work with ones that do. You have a track to ride on and the Ford Focus parts have been upgraded with all Mercedes components. You know how to understand and remember facts better. You possess more skills. You know how to learn better than most teens and young adults. Now, let's accelerate your learning even more.

The lessons included in Part 3 of this workbook are designed to help you learn much faster. Chances are you haven't tried or even heard of most of the strategies given here. The strategies and skills (like speed reading) contained in lessons 46 through 65 in Part 3 are more difficult to master and require you practice them a lot. But, they will give you the know how and the skills most adults don't have.

Work on mastering each skill separately. Once you're confident that you have the skills a particular lesson teaches, move on to the next one. Just be sure to consistently use of the skills as you learn them. This helps you develop a habit of using them every time. If you don't practice what you learn your body and mind will revert to the old, less-effective ways of learning.

Part 3 lessons are for those who have the will and the desire to become super-learners and super-achievers. Your future success will not depend on what you know right now. Your success will be determined by your ability to learn new things on the fly. As the amount of information grows exponentially, the demand grows for individuals who can learn things and gain skills needed to perform new jobs quickly. And whether they choose to work for someone else or for themselves, they will outperform the competition. They will crush school, work, and life.

This can be you. The next 60 pages will show you how. Just don't forget to use them. And keep using them because while a Mercedes is cool, a Tesla Roadster is where it's at.

Have fun and crush it.

LESSON 46 - 2 Cs OF ACCELERATED LEARNING

BIG QUESTIONS

1. How do feedback and competition drive progress?
2. How can you use feedback and competition to improve your performance?

ACTIVE READING

Read the passage below actively: 1) Preview, 2) Take Notes in the Margins, and 3) Summarize.

{START OF READING}

Competition elevates the craft. It makes breakthroughs possible. This is evident in sports. In the present, Golden Age of tennis, Roger Federer, Rafa Nadal, and Novak Djokovic continue pushing each other to new heights. In business, companies such as Apple and Samsung compete for our approval with their newest, baddest-to-date smartphones. The social media platforms, while competing against one another for our short attention spans, have us competing with our friends and followers on Facebook, Instagram, Twitter, and Snapchat for the title of "the most creative picture," or "the cleverest line," or "the most hilarious fail."

Undoubtedly, competition drives innovation. But growth through innovation only happens when feedback from the experiences - especially the losing ones - is absorbed and applied and the process, the product, or the person is improved.

Compete to Collect and Apply Feedback

Losing stinks. We hate losing because to lose at something means our hopes, plans, and goals go unfulfilled. Our brain wants to close the loop and it's hard to let something unfinished go. And losing is unfinished business. But we can be like Abe and use it to our advantage.

Abraham Lincoln, widely considered as one of the best US Presidents, lost 8 elections for various political offices. But instead of doing what most people do and giving up, he used his failures to improve. His eventual success can be attributed to 3 things:

1. Reading - he read incessantly and become a great communicator. This allowed him to compete.
2. Experience - he held different posts failing and succeeding in numerous professions and political elections. He competed and collected feedback.
3. Adaptation - he admitted his mistakes and owned his failures. He applied feedback to improve.

Would Lincoln be the leader he turned out to be if he did not compete and collect and apply feedback?

Treat Criticism as Coaching

They say "words can't hurt us" but it's untrue. Even if we don't show it, we care about what others think of us. It's a natural human reaction to want to be accepted and thought about as a good, or an intelligent, or an otherwise attractive person. It's instinctual.

But fighting instincts is often beneficial. The ability to absorb and carefully consider negative feedback and apply it can improve our performance. For example, you might get mad at your English teacher for bleeding red ink on the essay you put a lot of time into writing. You can think of her as a hater, be pissed for a while, and move on. Or, you can use it to improve. You can disagree with her but you can ask for more feedback to understand her point of view. You can ask her for suggestions on improving your essay. Because let's be real, the essay is good but not perfect. If you approach your teacher's negative feedback with an open mind, you will give yourself the opportunity to not only make your essay better but elevate your writing skill as well.

Continued on next page →

In this way, you can use someone else's criticisms and disagreements, regardless of their validity, to improve your past self and create a new and upgraded model. This is not saying you should act to satisfy your critics. Rather, use their words as feedback that helps you find the nuances of your "game" you can improve. Then, work on improving them. Maybe that's why LeBron James said *"I like criticism. It makes you strong."* Just as a coach can help you become stronger at a skill, criticism can prove priceless in pointing out the weaknesses of your "game" you were not aware of. And if you can find something to improve, you can find a way to improve it.

Intellectual friction - differing opinions and world views often manifested as criticisms and disagreements - is how most progress happens. This is why we collaborate with others. To make ideas better they must clash with other ideas - they must be challenged by others and viewed from many perspectives.

Accelerate Your Own Learning

You can accelerate your own growth and performance by being intentional. If you choose to continually "raise the bar" to push your limits, you will improve your skills. Want to get better at soccer? Pick a skill like dribbling, get feedback, and then practice that one skill repeatedly getting more feedback along the way. Then, you can move on to shooting and after that to something else. Do you want to draw better? Challenge yourself to draw something every day and pick one drawing microskill after another to work on improving and improve you will.

Most of the time, we are not intentional enough. We might want to get better at something, continue doing it over and over, and slowly improve. Once we reach a certain level of performance our progress halts. To achieve higher performance faster, you must become more intentional about self-improvement.

This involves 3 things. First, you have to challenge yourself to get incrementally better at something. Second, you need to come up with a plan to improve one little thing at a time. Third, you must follow your plan and apply new feedback when you receive it - you must be open to criticism and use it as feedback and you must find a way to compete, which will push you to new heights.

School, work, or life are no different. To become more successful, constantly challenge yourself to learn more, gain new skills, improve existing skills, and make more things applying this knowledge and skills. Think bigger today than you did yesterday. Competition and criticism will provide the necessary feedback. Follow feedback with action and you will accelerate your learning.

SUMMARY - Use your notes and understanding to answer the BIG QUESTIONS at the beginning of this lesson.

_____

_____

_____

_____

Give a 2-3 examples that apply to you of how you can use *Competition* to get better at learning.

_____

_____

_____

Give a 2-3 examples that apply to you of how you can use *Criticism* to get better at school.

_____

_____

_____

LESSON 47 - IMPROVE YOUR CRITICAL THINKING

BIG IDEAS

1. Why is critical thinking necessary for school and work success?
2. What are some ways you can improve your critical thinking?

QUICK COLLABORATION - Find a partner and discuss what critical thinking is and why it's important. Record below.

_____

_____

_____

_____

Look up the words Scrutiny and Skepticism and rephrase their definitions in your own words.

Scrutiny _____

Skepticism _____

EXAMINE AN INFOGRAPHIC OR WATCH A VIDEO

Go to *bit.ly/tcritic* to examine the infographic or to *bit.ly/critvid* to watch the video on Improving Critical Thinking. Then, name and describe each way/step of becoming a better critical thinker.

Step 1 is _____

It involves _____

_____

Step 2 is _____

It involves _____

_____

Step 3 is _____

It involves _____

_____

Step 4 is _____

It involves _____

_____

Step 5 is _____

It involves _____

_____

APPLY WHAT YOU LEARNED - Demonstrate the 5 critical thinking steps in solving the hypothetical problem below.

A smart female minority student enjoys participating in class discussions in political science. She is always prepared and her comments are supported by class materials but she feels more closely scrutinized than her classmates. She is repeatedly asked to defend everything she says and back it up with research by a male Caucasian student. He often cuts her off but does not seem to do this to other classmates.

Use the 5 steps of the critical thinking approach to decide:
1. Is this a case of discrimination?
2. What should she do about this unequal treatment?
3. Should the other students do something?
4. Is this treatment extreme enough to warrant being addressed by the instructor?

1. FORMULATE A QUESTION: *This is already done for you above with the 4 questions to answer.*

2. GATHER INFORMATION: _____
_____
_____
_____
_____

3. APPLY THE INFORMATION:
_____
_____
_____
_____

4. CONSIDER IMPLICATIONS: _____
_____
_____
_____

5. EXPLORE ALTERNATIVES:
_____
_____
_____
_____

LESSON REFLECTION - Explain how going through the 5-step critical thinking process affected your final decisions. Consider what your first impressions and initial reactions were and how they changed as a result of the process.

_____
_____
_____

LESSON 48 - CREATIVITY

BIG IDEA: Name habits anyone can develop to become more creative.

PERSONAL REFLECTION - Do you consider yourself to be creative? Explain.

_____

_____

_____

EXAMINE AN INFOGRAPHIC - Go to *bit.ly/growcreativity* and examine *The Creative Way Infographic*. Then, list the 8 Creativity Habits and provide a brief description for each.

1. _____

2. _____

3. _____

4. _____

5. _____

6. _____

7. _____

8. _____

APPLY IT - Use the drawing below to create a Memory Palace that helps you remember the 8 creativity habits. Use a different body part for each habit and describe the visualization that helps you remember what that habit is about. Follow the example of how HEAD/BRAIN was used to remember *SLEEP* to complete the memory palace.

HEAD/BRAIN = **1. SLEEP**. I'm imagining dreaming about being in a gallery full of paintings and then waking up and coming up with an idea for a new invention.

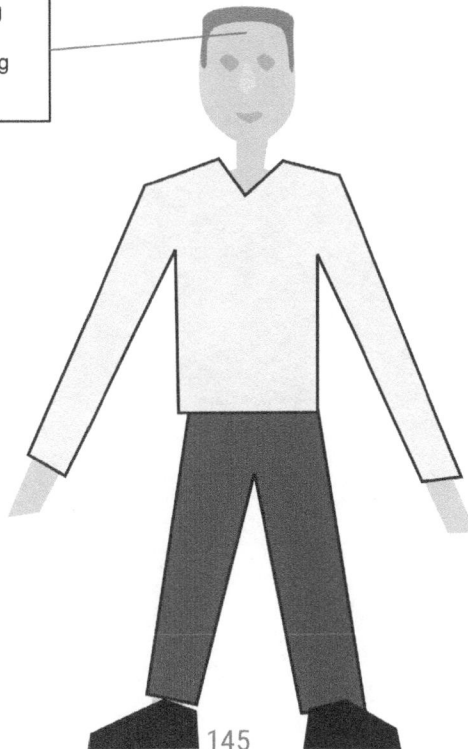

PRACTICE:

Find another person and tell him or her about the 8 Creativity Habits from memory using your memory palace. Give them an example for each.

LESSON REFLECTION - Explain how your ideas about creativity have changed during this lesson. How can you become more creative? What are 3 specific things you could do to practice creativity today, tomorrow, whenever?

LESSON 49 - INNOVATION

BIG IDEAS

1. What is innovation and how does most innovation happen?
2. What approaches can you use to become more innovative?

QUICK COLLABORATION - Discuss what it means to *Be Innovative* with a partner. Record your thoughts below.

_____

_____

_____

_____

_____

WATCH A VIDEO - Go to *bit.ly/engineofidea* and watch the ***Where Good Ideas Come From Video*** answering questions as they show up.

SUMMARIZE THE VIDEO by explaining where ideas come from, how they develop, and why this is the best time in history for innovation.

_____

_____

_____

_____

_____

_____

What role does curiosity and learning new things play in innovation? Explain with an example. Use visuals or words.

_____

_____

_____

_____

_____

_____

USING DESIGN THINKING TO INNOVATE - Go to *bit.ly/designt2* and examine the *Hacking Design Thinking for Education* **Infographic.** Then, complete the comic strip below that explains the five stages visually and using words.

EMPATHY	DEFINITION
IDEATION	**PROTOTYPING**
TESTING	**SUMMARY**

APPLY IT - Design a solution to the problem below using the Design Thinking Approach. Go through each step of the process carefully to propose an innovative solution. You can work solo or in a team.

The 600,000-square-mile Great Pacific Garbage Patch is a collection of plastic trash floating in the Pacific Ocean. The trash patch that's twice the size of Texas originates in North and South American and Asian countries and converges between Hawaii and California due to prevailing winds and ocean currents. The patch is not a solid mass of plastic. It includes about 1.8 trillion pieces and weighs 88,000 tons — the equivalent of 500 jumbo jets. Ocean pollution degrades water quality and leads to marine plant and animal deaths. The problem is, we depend on plastic. Since the '50s, we have produced 18.2 trillion pounds of plastic or the amount equal in size to 1 billion elephants. But something has to happen. We must first clean up the trash. Second, we must prevent plastics getting in the ocean. (Source: **USA Today**)

EMPATHY - Take into account regular people, governments, environment, and marine life.

What should you research to empathize? _____

_____

_____

_____

How could you engage in a similar experience? _____

_____

_____

What are the main problems? _____

_____

_____

What questions should you be asking people affected and yourself? _____

_____

_____

What else could you do to understand the problems better? _____

_____

_____

_____

DEFINITION - Identify how the problem and potential solutions impact all parties involved.

What is needed to begin solving this problem? _____

_____

_____

_____

_____

What are the different points of view on this? (regular people of different countries, scientists, governments etc.)

_____

_____

_____

_____

_____

_____

_____

Why and how might making changes be difficult? _____

_____

_____

_____

_____

_____

_____

IDEATION - Brainstorm ideas on your own first. Then, with your team, share, combine, and record all ideas.

Your ideas (come up with as many as you can. *Crazy, weird, outrageous etc. ideas are okay!*)

_____

_____

_____

_____

_____

Shared and Combined Team Ideas:

_____

_____

_____

_____

_____

_____

_____

_____

_____

PROTOTYPING - This isn't just about physical objects. You can prototype ideological solutions or plans of action. With your team, come up with 3 different experimental plans to solve the "Pacific Trash Patch" problem. Briefly describe them below.

Plan #1 _____

_____

_____

_____

_____

_____

PROTOTYPING CONTINUED...

Plan #2 _____

_____

_____

_____

_____

_____

_____

Plan #3 _____

_____

_____

_____

_____

_____

_____

TESTING - Pick at least one of the options below. Find and email or call and present your 3 prototypical ideas to:

Option 1: A scientist who's involved in the "Pacific Trash Patch" problem.

Option 2: A government contact who might have some say or be affected by this problem.

Option 3: A regular person who might be *directly* affected by this problem.

Option 4: A plastics company.

What was their feedback on your ideas? _____

_____

_____

_____

_____

_____

LESSON 50 - MASTERING DIFFICULT CONCEPTS

BIG IDEAS

1.   How can you use the Feynman Technique to master difficult concepts?

WATCH A VIDEO

Go to **bit.ly/feyntech** and watch the video on **The Feynman Technique**. Then, name and visually show what each step involves. Draw pictures and label and describe what happens in each.

Step 1 is _____

It looks like this:

Step 2 is _____

It looks like this:

Step 3 is _____

It looks like this:

Step 4 is _____

It looks like this:

APPLY IT! - Use the Feynman Technique to learn something difficult. Pick a topic from a class you're currently taking that you find difficult or impossible to grasp. If you find everything easy, ask your teacher or parent to suggest one to you. Ask them to give you an example from work or a book or an article they recently read.

Step 1: DECIDE ON A TOPIC

What is the topic? _____

Write down everything you know about it now:

_____

_____

_____

_____

_____

_____

_____

_____

_____

_____

_____

_____

_____

What are the 3 sources you can learn about this topic from?

1. _____

2. _____

3. _____

Go to all 3 of those sources and learn something new from each about this topic. Add what you learned above.

Step 2: EXPLAIN WHAT YOU WROTE DOWN

Find someone to explain what you wrote down to. Break it down into simpler concepts and provide examples. Below, note the things that were difficult to explain because you had a hard time understanding them completely yourself.

_____

_____

_____

_____

_____

Step 3: FILL IN THE GAPS

1. Review the parts you still don't understand, find fuzzy, and have a hard time explaining.

2. Go back to your sources and find information that explains your "knowledge gaps."

3. Learn to fill in those gaps.

4. Again, try to explain them to someone else or to yourself. You might have to go to more than one source to form complete understanding and that's okay. The worst thing is to give up right before you have it!

Step 4: SIMPLIFY & USE ANALOGIES

1. If there is any jargon (technical terms) used, simplify the language by changing the jargon to simple language.

2. Use analogies that help you compare or contrast this new, difficult concept to something you (and everyone else) can relate to. Think about what the concept seems like or is similar to. What does it remind you of?

3. Explain it to someone else again using the tips above. If you're still struggling with explaining it in simple terms, it means you still don't fully understand it. Once you are able to do so you will know YOU GOT THIS!

LESSON 51 - MATH & SCIENCE PROBLEM SOLVING

BIG IDEAS

1. How should your learning approach to math, science, and similar subjects be different from other subjects?
2. What is an effective approach to problem solving?

ACTIVE READING

Read the following excerpt from *Chapter 4: Use The Right Method* of the book *Crush School 2*. Read actively by previewing, taking margin notes, and summarizing.

{START OF READING}

What you'll learn: Every subject requires a unique learning approach. It's best to figure out how to learn something before you learn it. There'll be examples!

Use the Right Method

I often see chemistry students trying to memorize chemistry definitions. This approach might work for a vocab quiz. But what if I change how these definitions are worded? The words mean the same thing, but are different. Psych! I don't mean to be evil, but I want my students to understand concepts. I want them to be able to figure things out.

I hope you have teachers who do that too, because if they just feed you information and ask you to repeat it, they are setting you up for a future full of disappointments. It's because no matter what you end up doing for work, you'll have to be able to figure things out; and not just to solve problems, but also come up with creative solutions. And you just can't learn this by repeating what some book says.

To solve a problem, you need to understand the problem first, often from multiple perspectives, and then you must know how to begin solving it. You need the right approach.

There's a method to this madness they say, because the approach you choose has to fit the problem you face. Same goes for learning. It makes little sense to approach learning chemistry the same way you study history, right? It might seem obvious, but I see students try and fail to apply what works in one class to another all the time.

It doesn't work. Always ask yourself: *What am I learning and what's the best way to learn it?* If you don't know, ask your teacher what she recommends or just google *the best way to study* _____.

I don't want to leave you hanging here, so I'll give you some subject specific examples.

If you're learning **chemistry**, say solving **stoichiometry** problems, write down the steps your teacher, book, or the web gives first. Then, look at example problems and learn to identify each step. It's key to understand what each step actually does, so think about it. Next, solve problems on your own, identifying each step and knowing where you are in the process. You can start by solving problems and looking at examples as you do it. The end goal is to get to the point where you understand the steps and can do them on your own.

Continued on next page →

Learning **math** or **physics** is similar to stoichiometry. You might have a fewer or more steps and formulas to use, but you always want to understand what you're doing. Mindless repetition is for zombies.

If it's science, business, or social studies **concepts** you need to master, the best strategy is to use them somehow. You might explain how mitosis works in your own words to a younger sibling or create a business plan for your future ice cream joint. Drawing a comic and using it to explain a historical event or recording a video comparing and contrasting US and Canada will help you remember these things better than reading and rereading text about them.

Need to change your **car's oil**? YouTube. Pop the hood. Crawl under.

And now the obvious, but not so obvious, and super useful hack.

Humans have one really stupid expectation of themselves: *We expect to know something before we even learn it.*

I do it all the time. Looking back, I could have saved a lot of time and frustration by being smarter and asking others questions. So... If you are having trouble figuring something out on your own, get used to asking for help. Most people are happy to help. They welcome questions, because it lets them shine. Experts want to use their know how. Otherwise, what's the point of having knowledge and skills?

Problem is we're not asking. We just go it alone. Dumb, isn't it?

In a perfect school, teachers would teach the important stuff; the things you can use and care about right now. I'll admit that a lot of stuff I teach in chemistry is useless. There are things though, that might help in the future. Which ones? I'd tell you if I knew.

I hope education is heading in the direction of teaching more of the things you want to learn and fewer of the noise variety, but in the meantime, you can learn how to figure everything out.

Chapter Summary

The point is that if you learn how to figure out the best method to learn a concept or skill, you'll become a quicker learner, but getting this process going may be slow and frustrating at first. Each subject is different and requires its own approach. Sometimes the tweaks are small and sometimes huge. The struggle is real, but if you have the chops for it, you will come out on top.

Jedi who knows the way, strong is the force with him. - Yoda

SUMMARY _____

_____

_____

_____

_____

LESSON 52 - MAKE BETTER DECISIONS

BIG IDEAS

1. Why is it important to consider a problem from multiple perspectives?
2. What strategies can you use to make better-informed decisions?

QUICK COLLABORATION - Find a partner and talk about how you reach decisions. What process do you follow?

_____

_____

_____

EXAMINE AN INFOGRAPHIC

Go to *bit.ly/6hatway* and examine the *Making Decisions Using The 6 Thinking Hats Infographic*. Then, explain in your own words what decision perspective each hat symbolizes.

WHITE HAT _____

_____

RED HAT _____

_____

BLACK HAT _____

_____

YELLOW HAT _____

_____

GREEN HAT _____

_____

BLUE HAT _____

_____

THINK ABOUT IT - What types of decisions could the 6 hat approach help you with? Where could you see yourself using it? Give at least 3 specific examples.

_____

_____

_____

_____

_____

_____

APPLY IT! - Use the 6 hat decision-making approach to solve the conundrum below. Good luck!

Your best friend and you promised each other at the beginning of your senior year that you will go to the prom without dates but rather you'll go together and hang out together. But yesterday, two weeks before the prom a cute guy (or girl) you secretly like has asked you to be his (or her) date to the prom. You showed interest and thanked him/her but told him/her that though you want to go with him/her you will need a couple of days to make your decision. It's getting really close to decision time. You don't want to hurt your best friend but are afraid the cute boy (or girl) who asked you out might ask someone else. What do you do? What does each hat tell you?

WHITE HAT _____

_____

_____

_____

RED HAT _____

_____

_____

_____

BLACK HAT _____

_____

_____

_____

YELLOW HAT _____

_____

_____

GREEN HAT _____

_____

_____

_____

BLUE HAT _____

_____

_____

_____

LESSON 53 - READ FASTER #1

BIG IDEAS

1. What are 2 main ways in which a visual pacer helps you read faster?

LISTEN TO THE KWIK BRAIN PODCAST #7: <u>HOW TO READ FASTER</u>

Go to *bit.ly/readfast1* and listen. Use the **Take Notes / Make Notes** strategy below as you listen to the podcast.

Take Notes	Make Notes

SUMMARY:

5 MINUTE BRAIN BREAK

TEST & INCREASE YOUR READING SPEED - EXERCISE

The best way to get better at something is to first figure out your current performance at this task and then improve it with practice. Reading speed can and should be improved because if you do it the right way you'll be able to read articles and books faster and remember more of what you read.

ROUND 1: Read the passage below for **60 seconds** the way you've always done. Set your alarm to 60 seconds and go. Stop after the alarm sounds and count the number of lines you read. BEGIN READING BELOW (or you can use a class textbook or a book you're currently reading).

READING: SPEED READING FOR DUMMIES CHEAT SHEET

From **Speed Reading For Dummies** By Richard Sutz, Peter Weverka

You can use speed reading to enhance both your reading ability and your reading enjoyment. Some misconceptions about the speed reading method persist — pay no attention to them. By making slight adjustments to your reading habits, especially stopping yourself from hearing or saying each word, you can move from being an average reader with average comprehension to a proficient speed-reader with excellent comprehension.

See Where You Stand As A Speed Reader

If you're challenging yourself to become a speed reader, you may be curious to know how you compare to others in the speed-reading department. (And who wouldn't be?) Roughly speaking, readers fall into these categories where speed is concerned:

- 1 to 200 WPM (words per minute): You're a talker. You read one word at a time at about the same speed as you talk and you may move your lips when you read. Most talkers are held back because they engage in *vocalization* while they read — they speak the words silently to themselves as they read them. Unless you're an especially fast talker, reading at the speed you talk slows you down.
- 200 to 300 WPM: You're an average reader, one who probably doesn't enjoy reading as a hobby. You engage in some vocalization as you read, but you can read several words at once. Most people read at this speed.
- 300 to 700 WPM: You're an above average reader who can read groups of words in a single glance, recognizing and reading phrases in sentences quickly. You vocalize a little when you read. You very likely have a large vocabulary.
- 700+ WPM: You're a speed reader. You're adept at reading 10 to 16 words at a glance, both horizontally and vertically on the page. You read with a great degree of confidence and agility.

So if you read 700 or more words per minute, take the rest of the day off. You don't need speed--reading lessons — you're already a fast reader.

Defining Speed Reading

Speed reading isn't a whole different way of reading; it's just a more focused way of reading. Reading engages the eyes, ears, mouth, and, of course, the brain. Speed reading engages these senses even more than normal reading because you use your senses and brain power even more efficiently.

NUMBER OF LINES READ NORMALLY _____

ROUND 2: Use a **visual pacer** such as a **pencil** or **finger** and read the passage below for **60 seconds**. Start your timer and go. Stop after the 60-second alarm sounds and count the number of lines you read. BEGIN READING BELOW (or use a class textbook or book you're currently reading).

READING: SPEED READING FOR DUMMIES CHEAT SHEET

From **Speed Reading For Dummies** By Richard Sutz, Peter Weverka

Speed Reading Is...

- Seeing: The first step in reading anything is seeing the words. With speed reading, you use your sight in specific ways:
    - You read several words in a single glance. Unless you're encountering words you don't know or haven't read before, you don't read words one at a time.
    - You expand your vision so that you can read and understand many words in a single glance. A very good speed reader can read, see, and process 10 to 14 words at once.
    - You expand your vision to read vertically as well as horizontally on the page. Speed readers can read and understand words on two or three different lines in a single glance.
- Silent reading: Most people hear words when they read. You may speak words to yourself because you learned to read with the sound-it-out method. The problem with sounding out words when you read is that you read not at the speed you think but rather at the speed you talk. Sounding it out is fine for beginning readers, but at some point you have to dispense with sound if you want to be a speed reader. Saying the words, even if you only whisper them inside the confines of your skull, takes time and prevents you from reading as fast as you can.
- Decoding the words: When you come across a word in your reading that you don't know or recognize, you have to decode it. You break it into syllables, try to pronounce it, and see whether it's related to words you know. You try to get its meaning, and if you can't do that on your own, you consult a dictionary or other reference source. The more you read, the fewer words you have to decode because reading enlarges your vocabulary. It introduces you to more words.
- Comprehending: The purpose of reading is to comprehend — to learn something new, see the world from a different perspective, or maybe just get information to pass an exam or prepare for a business meeting. How well you comprehend what you read is determined by your
    - Reading speed: When you don't read at the right speed, your comprehension is diminished. One of the skills you acquire as a speed reader is knowing when to slow down and when to speed up. The fastest speed readers adjust the speed at which they read, just as the fastest stock car racers slow down when they're in a crowded field or on a slick patch of roadway. They adjust their speed according to the type of reading they're doing.
    - Breadth of vocabulary: Having a large vocabulary is a must for speed readers. You can't get away from it.
    - Degree of familiarity with the subject matter: How strong a background you have in the topic you're reading about determines how well you comprehend what you read. Obviously, you have a head start if you're traveling in territory you're familiar with and you know the jargon already.
- Concentrating: All reading requires a certain amount of concentration. Speed reading, however, requires sustained, forceful concentration because when you speed read, you do many things at once. As you see and read the words on the page, you also remain alert to the main ideas that the author wants to present. You have to think along with the author and detect how she presents the material so you can pin down the main ideas.
- As you read, you have to read with more perspective and separate the details from weightier stuff. You have to know when to skim, when to read fast, and when to slow down to get the gist of it.

NUMBER OF LINES READ USING A VISUAL PACER _____

Check Your Results On The Next Page→

DID YOU READ FASTER?

Number of lines you read during the **1st reading**	Number of lines you read during the **2nd reading**	Divide **2nd/1st**	Multiply by **100**	Subtract **100**. This is how many % faster (or slower) you read

Your Result _____

REFLECT

Did you read faster? Why (or why not) do you think this happened?

_____

_____

What are 2-3 things you can do to increase and keep increasing your reading speed?

_____

_____

_____

_____

LESSON 54 - READ FASTER #2

BIG IDEAS

1. Why is complete elimination of subvocalizing impossible?
2. What are 5 ways to minimize subvocalizing?

WHAT IS SUBVOCALIZATION? VIDEO

1. READ 1-7 BEFORE WATCHING.
2. Watch the **What Is SUBVOCALIZATION?** video by going to **bit.ly/subvocalize**.
3. Pay attention to the definition and description of subvocalization.
4. Go to settings (the gear to the right of CC), change the speed to 0.5 and watch the first 48 seconds.
5. Now, go to settings again, change the speed to 1.5, focus, and watch the first 48 seconds.
6. Again, go to settings, change the speed to 1.0, and watch the first 48 seconds.
7. Experiment with other speeds to find the speed that allows you to maintain your best focus.

YOUR IMPRESSIONS

Were you surprised? Explain.

_____

_____

Which speed was most distracting? _____

Which speed helped you focus best? _____

How can you use this new found information when learning?

_____

_____

Why does Subvocalizing while reading slow you down?

_____

_____

5 MINUTE BRAIN BREAK

ACTIVE READING & NOTE-TAKING

Read the passage on the next page by IRiS Reading's Paul Nowak. Preview, Read, and Take Notes on key ideas.

5 WAYS TO MINIMIZE SUBVOCALIZATION

1. Use Your Hand to Guide Your Eyes While Reading

We keep on emphasizing the importance of using your hand to guide your eyes. It's a central principle to all speed-reading techniques and it's something that will help you minimize subvocalization. Using your hand to guide your eyes will also help you grab groups of words while reading, helping you avoid another common reading habit, fixation.

2. Distract Yourself

To minimize subvocalization, try distracting yourself from saying words in your head. How should you distract yourself? There are a couple of ways to do it. One way is try to chew gum while you read. If you chew gum while reading it will distract you from saying the words in your head.

You can also distract yourself from saying words by occupying that voice in your head with another voice. Try counting from one to three while you are reading the material (example: "one, two three" line-by-line). While you are doing this, try fixating your eyes somewhere at the beginning of the line, somewhere in the middle of the line, and somewhere at the end of the line. While you are looking in those three places you want to be counting "one, two, three." By doing this you will also be fixating on three groups of words, rather than each and every single word. You can count "one, two, three" out loud (maybe whispering) or in your head. Either way, you'll distract yourself from saying the actual words you are reading. With some practice, you'll find it easier to avoid saying all the words in your head as you read.

3. Listen To Music While Reading

This will not only help you minimize subvocalization, but listening to music may also help you concentrate better. However, keep in mind that not all types of music are going to help you concentrate. You want to avoid listening to music with lyrics or anything with a strong beat because it is going to throw off your concentration. You may also want to avoid listening to songs that remind you of other things (your high school sweetheart, a fight scene from a movie or anything else that might further distract you).

Listen to something that is instrumental. Classical music usually works best. That will help you to improve your concentration and it will also help you to minimize your habit of subvocalization.

4. Use the AccelaReader RSVP Application

AccelaReader uses Rapid Serial Visual Presentation (RSVP) to help you boost your reading speed and minimize subvocalization. The application is simple to use. You simply paste the text you want to read into a textbox. Set your reading speed and press play. The words then blink on the screen at the speed that you set. You can also choose how many words you want to blink at a time. I recommend setting a speed of at least 300 words per minute. Anything higher than that will help you avoid subvocalizing all the words. The faster you go, the less words you will be able to say in your head. With some practice, you'll find it easier to minimize this habit of subvocalization.

5. Force Yourself To Read Faster Than You Normally Would

Let's say you normally read 250 wpm. Try going a little faster (maybe 300 or 350 wpm). If you force yourself to go a little faster than you normally read, you'll minimize the amount of words you say in your head. In addition to minimizing subvocalization, you'll also improve your focus because you have to pay attention more when you read a little faster. Again, the more you practice pushing yourself faster, the faster you will get.

Use the **Take Notes / Make Notes** strategy below as you read

Take Notes	Make Notes

SUMMARY:

LESSON 55 - READ FASTER #3

BIG IDEAS

1. Why does subvocalizing slow down the reading speed?
2. How can you minimize subvocalizing?

LISTEN TO THE KWIK BRAIN PODCAST #13: 3 HACKS FOR RAPID READING (HOW TO REDUCE SUBVOCALIZATION)

Go to *bit.ly/readfast2* and listen. Use the **Take Notes / Make Notes** strategy below as you listen to the podcast.

Take Notes	Make Notes

SUMMARY:

TEST & INCREASE YOUR READING SPEED - EXERCISE #2

The best way to read faster is to first figure out your current speed and then practice to improve it. The more you practice, the more you improve. You can practice EVERY SINGLE TIME YOU READ.

ROUND 1: Read the passage below for **60 seconds** using a visual pacer such as a **pencil** or **finger**. Set your alarm to 60 seconds. Stop after the alarm sounds and count the number of lines you read. BEGIN READING BELOW (or use a class textbook or book you're currently reading).

Speed Reading Tips: 5 Ways to Minimize Subvocalization by Paul Nowak

Subvocalization (also known as auditory reassurance) is a very common habit among readers. It involves saying words in your head while reading and it's one of the main reasons why people read slowly and have trouble improving their reading speed.

Many speed-reading programs tend to exaggerate and will falsely claim that the key to speed reading is to eliminate the habit of subvocalization. However, study after study shows that eliminating this habit completely is not possible.

In this article, we will discuss how you can minimize subvocalization – not eliminate it. Minimizing subvocalization will help you boost your reading speed, and it will also help you improve your comprehension.

Are You Hearing Your Own Voice in Your Head?

If you're hearing yourself in your head while reading, that is because this is how most people were taught to read; to say the words silently in their head.

When you were initially taught to read, you were told to read out loud. Once you were fluent enough, your teacher probably told you to start saying the words in your head. This is how the habit of subvocalization usually originates. Most people continue reading this way for the rest of their lives. But if you want to start reading faster, you need to minimize this habit.

You don't need to say every word in your head to be able to understand what you are reading. When you were younger, it was absolutely necessary to say each and every single word, but now you can extract the meaning of words by simply seeing them. You don't need to pronounce them, out loud or in your head, to get that same understanding.

Here's an example of what I mean. Think about when you are driving. When you see a stop sign, do you actually vocalize the word "STOP" in your head? You may have done so right now while reading the words in the sentence, but when you see a stop sign while driving you're unlikely to say the word. You see it and recognize that it's a stop sign automatically.

If you're like most readers, you probably subvocalize all or most of the words in your head. But you don't always vocalize everything you read. Here's another example of this: if you were reading and came across the year "1977", you probably wouldn't vocalize in your head "Nineteen Seventy-Seven." You would be more likely to understand the year by just seeing the number. Or if you saw the number "3,472,382,977", you probably wouldn't vocalize the words "three billion, four hundred seventy-two million, three hundred eighty-two thousand, nine hundred and seventy-seven." That's a mouthful. For a number like that, you see it and know it's a big one. The understanding comes quickly. You don't subvocalize it. If you did, you'd be staring at that number for a while without making progress through the sentence.

NUMBER OF LINES READ IN ROUND 1 _____

ROUND 2: Use a **visual pacer** again and read the passage below for **60 seconds**. This time, **stay aware of your lips moving or the voice in your head** saying the words as you read and **try to turn it off**. Stop after the 60-second alarm sounds and count the number of lines you read. BEGIN READING BELOW (or use a class textbook or book you're currently reading).

It Isn't About Words, It's About Ideas

Reading isn't even about words but rather about extracting ideas, absorbing information, and getting details. Words by themselves don't mean much unless they're surrounded by other words. When you read the words "New York City", do you even think of it as three words? If you're like most people, you would equate those three words (New York City) to a city. NYC would mean the same thing, right?

Many of the words we see are simply there for grammatical purposes (the, a, an). They don't provide you with the same kind of meaning as words like "university". We have to minimize subvocalization in order to boost our reading speed. Why do we have to do this? Because subvocalization limits how fast we can really read.

Think about it this way: if you are saying every word in your head, doesn't that mean that you can only read as fast as you can talk? If you're saying every single word in your head, your limit is going to be your talking speed.

Reading Speed = Talking Speed for Most People

The average reading speed is about 150-250 words per minute (wpm). And the average talking speed is exactly the same. Because most people say words in their head while reading (subvocalization), they tend to read at around the same rate as they talk. You can test this out for yourself if you like. Try reading for one minute normally, and then try reading out loud for one minute. If you're like most people, your reading speed and talking speed will be similar (within 50 words higher or lower).

Why do most people read between 150 and 250 wpm and not above 300 wpm? Because it's hard to talk that fast. Unless you do disclaimers at the end of commercials, it's difficult to talk over 300 words per minute. So subvocalization must be minimized because you don't want to get stuck reading as fast as you talk. You're capable of reading as fast as you can think.

Changing the habit of subvocalization is easier said than done. You can't just turn this voice in your head off. Instead of eliminating this habit, you want to minimize it. For example, let's say you're reading some text that said, "The boy jumped over the fence." To minimize subvocalization, you might just say in your head, "Boy jumped fence," three words rather than six words in that sentence. Some people think this means skipping words, but you are not actually skipping them. Your eyes still see all the other words. You are simply just saying a few of the words. This is how you minimize subvocalization.

Keep in mind that there are a lot of words in sentences and paragraphs that are not essential to the meaning of that paragraph. We are reading for ideas, not words.

NUMBER OF LINES READ IN ROUND 2 _____

Check Your Results On The Next Page→

DID YOU READ FASTER?

Number of lines you read during the *1st reading*	Number of lines you read during the *2nd reading*	Divide *2nd/1st*	Multiply by *100*	Subtract *100*. This is how many % faster (or slower) you read

Your Result _____

REFLECT

Did you read faster? Why (or why not) do you think this happened?

_____

_____

Did you find it easy to stop mouthing words or subvocalizing in your head? _____

Why is minimizing the voice in your head difficult?

_____

_____

_____

What are 2-3 things you can do to minimize subvocalizing?

_____

_____

_____

_____

LESSON 56 - MEET THE REAL YOU (YOUR CHRONOTYPE)

BIG IDEAS

1. What are chronotypes?
2. How can identifying your chronotype be helpful in learning and life?

ACTIVE READING

Read the article based on the *Chapter: Meet the Real You* from the book *Finding Time When You Have None*. Read Actively: 1) Preview, 2) Take Notes in the Margins, and 3) Summarize.

{START OF READING}

Dr. Michael Breus, the sleep doctor, uses four animals: Bear, Dolphin, Lion, and Wolf to describe four types of people and how the combination of our biology and the time of day influences our focus and productivity. They're called chronotypes. According to Dr. Breus, identifying your chronotype will help you identify the optimal times for your brain to do focused work and execute better as a result.

Figuring out your chronotype and learning about using it to your advantage will help you make more informed, strategic choices about when to work on the really heavy school work - the stuff that makes you want to stab your brain through your ear with the pencil you're holding, and the material and tasks you can handle more easily.

The 4 Chronotypes

Most people are *bears*. They sleep well and maintain energy throughout the day but typically need to recharge in the mid-afternoon to be able to stay productive into the evening hours.

Dolphins often lack a regular sleep routine and wake up during the night. Their most productive time is from mid-morning through early afternoon.

Lions are early-risers and do their best work before lunch time. They tend to wake up early, hustle hard 'til noon, and then start winding down. They're usually the first to go to bed.

Wolves hunt at lunchtime and howl at night. They execute at their best from 12-2 pm and from late afternoon into the night.

If you're not sure which chronotype you are, take the 45-second quiz at ***thepowerofwhenquiz.com*** to find out. And don't get stuck trying to fit one type - it's possible you are a chronotype combination, like a wolf in sheep's clothing, or maybe a lion in a dolphin's skin. Meet the real you. Then, use this information to optimize you.

SUMMARY - Explain why knowing your chronotype is beneficial.

_____

_____

_____

Which chronotype are you? _____ Explain _____

_____

APPLY IT

When do you usually study? Write down all the times you can think of. _____

_____

According to your chronotype, what are the best times for you to study? _____

_____

What are your hard, more mentally-demanding subjects?

_____   _____   _____

_____   _____   _____

What are your lighter subjects?

_____   _____   _____

_____   _____   _____

Come up with a quick plan of how you can modify your work time to fit your chronotype. Focus on finding time during your most effective hours. Reflect on your subjects: Which ones are easy enough for you to do anytime? Which ones require the most concentration and mental power? Put them down below.

Example: *Study math right after school (a Dolphin who finds math hard might do this).*

1. _____

2. _____

3. _____

4. _____

5. _____

6. _____

7. _____

8. _____

9. _____

LESSON 57 - BUILDING MEMORY PALACES

BIG IDEAS

1. Why is the Memory Palace method so powerful for storing information in your long-term memory?
2. How do you build an effective memory palace?

ACTIVE READING

Read the passage below to learn about the powerful Memory Palace method. Remember to (1) Preview. (2) Take Notes in the Margins, and (3) Summarize.

{START OF READING}

Do you know Austin? No, not your friend Austin but Austin Baio. Of course you don't. Few people do. Actually, about 74,000 do - this is how many hits his YouTube video reached in 2 years. In the video, 11-year-old Austin recites the first 2091 digits of π (pi). Yes, he MEMORIZED THE FIRST 2091 NUMBERS IN PI. *That's impressive!* you might say, and it is. Except 69-year-old memory champion Akira Haraguchi from Japan memorized the first 111,700 numbers of the neverending string you get when you divide a circle's circumference by its diameter.

And in case you're wondering, neither Austin nor Akira is a freak. They just know a powerful way to store all those digits in their long-term memory. They know how to create and use perhaps the most powerful memory technique called the Memory Palace method. And while you might not have a burning desire or need to memorize thousands of numbers, your learning, school, and life success will greatly benefit from your ability to use the Memory Palace method.

But before we get into building your first memory palace, let's talk about why this method crushes almost every other memory technique. If you remember *Chapter 15: The Learning Styles Myth* then you know that we learn best by using multiple senses and strategies when receiving and trying to remember new information. And guess what? Memory Palaces help you do just that - they tap into the power of your imagination and visual memory, they make effective use of emotions, and allow you to use hearing and touch as well - all designed to help you learn and remember large amounts of information in a relatively short amount of time.

Because there's no limit to the amount of stuff your brain can store, once you start building memory palaces your brain will become like a bank that contains many vaults. Inside each unique vault, your brain bank will store the information you deposit. Make frequent deposits and visits to the vaults - create many memory palaces and tour them - and you will remember more of what you learn. And it will be fun!

Don't believe me? Imagine your favorite cartoon character, maybe Spongebob, sitting on your living room couch drinking ice tea and smiling wide helping you remember that annoying chemistry term. Or Princess Elsa aiding you in mastering that key political science term while saving the world from evil princes. Or Wolverine slashing Deadpool to pieces while Thor is flying around fighting the Hulk and Iron Man is getting punched in the face by Captain America all with the goal of helping you learn parts of the cell for biology. If you're like *Dude... I get it.*

Another cool thing is you can use memory palaces to remember anything. A few school suggestions are:
- Main concepts (from lectures, readings, videos etc.)
- All kinds of vocabulary (English or foreign)
- Technical terms and programming code
- Class presentations (you have to give or someone gives)
- Numbers (dates, phone numbers, addresses, equations, constants etc.)
- Names (classmates and historical figures)

HOW TO BUILD A MEMORY PALACE

The "Palace" in Memory Palace is a location. This can be a building or a place or even a thing you know in detail. For example, you can use your room and specific objects in your room to memorize 10 vocabulary terms for a quiz. If you need to remember a lot of concepts for a big test, it makes more sense to use your entire apartment (or house) and the objects it contains to build your memory palace.

How big and how detailed your memory palace is depends on how much information you need to memorize.

Example 1. College Campus

1. You could use Building 427 if you know it well and pick 10 locations (entryway, main hallway, bathroom, specific rooms, food court etc.) to use for placing information you have to remember.

2. Or, if you need to remember a lot, build a memory palace by numbering Building 440 as "1," the grass area on top of it "2," the bigger grass area on top of it "3," Building 438 as "4," the trapezoid grass area next to it as "5," the bigger trapezoid area to the left would be "6," and so on until you get to Building 426, or number "22."

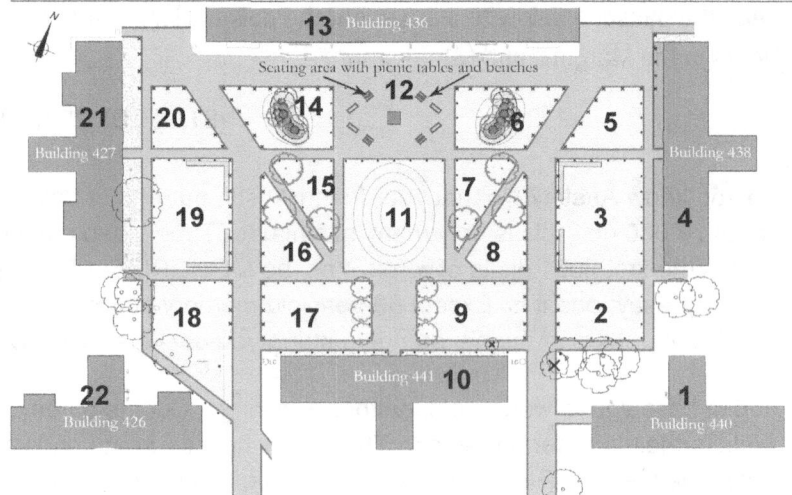

Example 2. Small Apartment

Depending on how much information you need to remember you can use the apartment only, or create a memory palace that includes the courtyard.

1. Number the lawn "1," the bushes on the bottom "2," the table "3," the bushes on top "4," the door "5, and so on using the inside."
2. Or number similarly to how the picture objects are numbered using couches, the table, the sink, the countertops, the bathtub, the beds etc. Try to use only large objects.

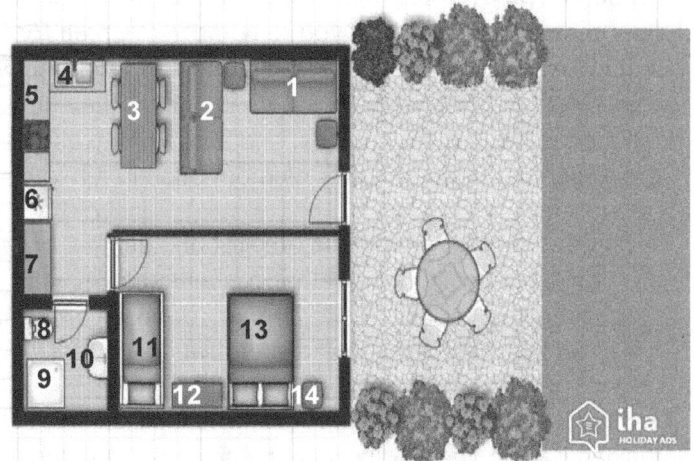

THINGS TO REMEMBER WHEN BUILDING MEMORY PALACES

1. Use entire spaces or large objects because small ones are too easy to move and forget.
2. Number in a way that prevents walking back and forth and crossing your path.
3. Practice the walk in your mind starting at the beginning, end, and middle (it's quick and fun).
4. Use locations you know well when learning how to use Memory Palaces. Later, you'll need new locations.
5. Use one location to remember one set of information. For example, do not reuse your home for a history test information if you previously used it to memorize your psychology presentation.

5 MINUTE BRAIN BREAK

BUILD YOUR FIRST MEMORY PALACE

1.   **Start with location.** You can use buildings and such - your room, your home, your place of work, the museum, the park, the store, the library, the school, your favorite restaurant or cafe, your body etc. In the beginning, pick locations you know well and can visualize easily - be able to close your eyes and mentally walk through and recreate what this place looks like and where the big objects in each room etc. are.

Write down 10 locations you know well _____

_____

_____

2.   **Pick one of the 10 locations** above: _____

3.   **Draw the floor plan** below. Model it on the example to the right. Don't worry about making it perfect - a rough sketch works. Make it large enough to write stuff in but you don't need to label what each room or space is. You already know it well.

4.   **Draw the walking path.** You don't have to start at the front door. Pick a path that is simple, does not cross or go back and forth.

5.   **Number.** If the place has 10+ rooms number them 1-10 or number 5 big objects in the first room 1-5, then 6-10 in the next room and so on. In the future, you can decide based on how many terms or concepts you must learn and remember for a quiz or test.

6.   **Practice walking your path in your mind.** Look away and mentally walk from the beginning to the end 2-3 times. Then, start at the end and retrace your steps all the way to the beginning 3 times. Then start in the middle and walk to the end. Then, walk form the middle to the beginning.

Your Floor Plan

USE THE SPACE BELOW TO DRAW A DIFFERENT OR BIGGER MEMORY PALACE

LESSON 58 - FILLING MEMORY PALACES

BIG IDEAS

1. How do you fill a Memory Palace?
2. How do you create associations?

WATCH A VIDEO: How to Memorize Fast and Easily // Mind Palace: Build a Memory Palace

Go to *bit.ly/mem_palace* and watch the video. Pause when necessary and use the space below to take notes. Focus on getting the information that helps you understand, build, and use Memory (or Mind) Palaces.

Video Notes	Your Interpretation

Summary:

_____

_____

_____

_____

FILL YOUR MEMORY PALACE: Go back to the drawing of your memory palace and follow the directions below to fill it. If needed, rewatch the video.

If you have a quiz or test coming up, you can use the vocab terms you have to know. List and number them below:

_____   _____   _____

_____   _____   _____

_____   _____   _____

_____   _____   _____

_____   _____   _____

_____   _____   _____

Otherwise, use these 10 chemistry terms: **1) atom, 2) proton, 3) neutron, 4) valence electron, 5) energy level, 6) cation, 7) anion, 8) octet rule, 9) ionic bond**, and **10) covalent bond**.

You numbered either the rooms or 5 big objects in each room in the previous lesson. Now, place your terms (or the chemistry ones) in this memory palace you drew yesterday. Make sure the numbers match.

Now, list and number 10+ characters you can _visualize easily_ to put in your palace. Mine are **1) Iron Man, 2) Smiley Face, 3) Roger Federer, 4) Thor, 5) The Hulk, 6) Professor Xavier, 7) Magneto, 8) Octopus, 9) James Bond, 10) Spongebob**. I was strategic about my picks and you can be too. The more images and associations between the characters and the concepts your mind can create the better. But, as you will see, picking any 10 characters without thinking about it too much will work as well. The more Memory Palaces you build and use the better you'll get at it.

_____   _____   _____

_____   _____   _____

_____   _____   _____

_____   _____   _____

_____   _____   _____

_____   _____   _____

Now, write each character's name next to the term/concept in your memory palace. Numbers must match!

CHECK OUT WHAT MY PALACE LOOKS LIKE:

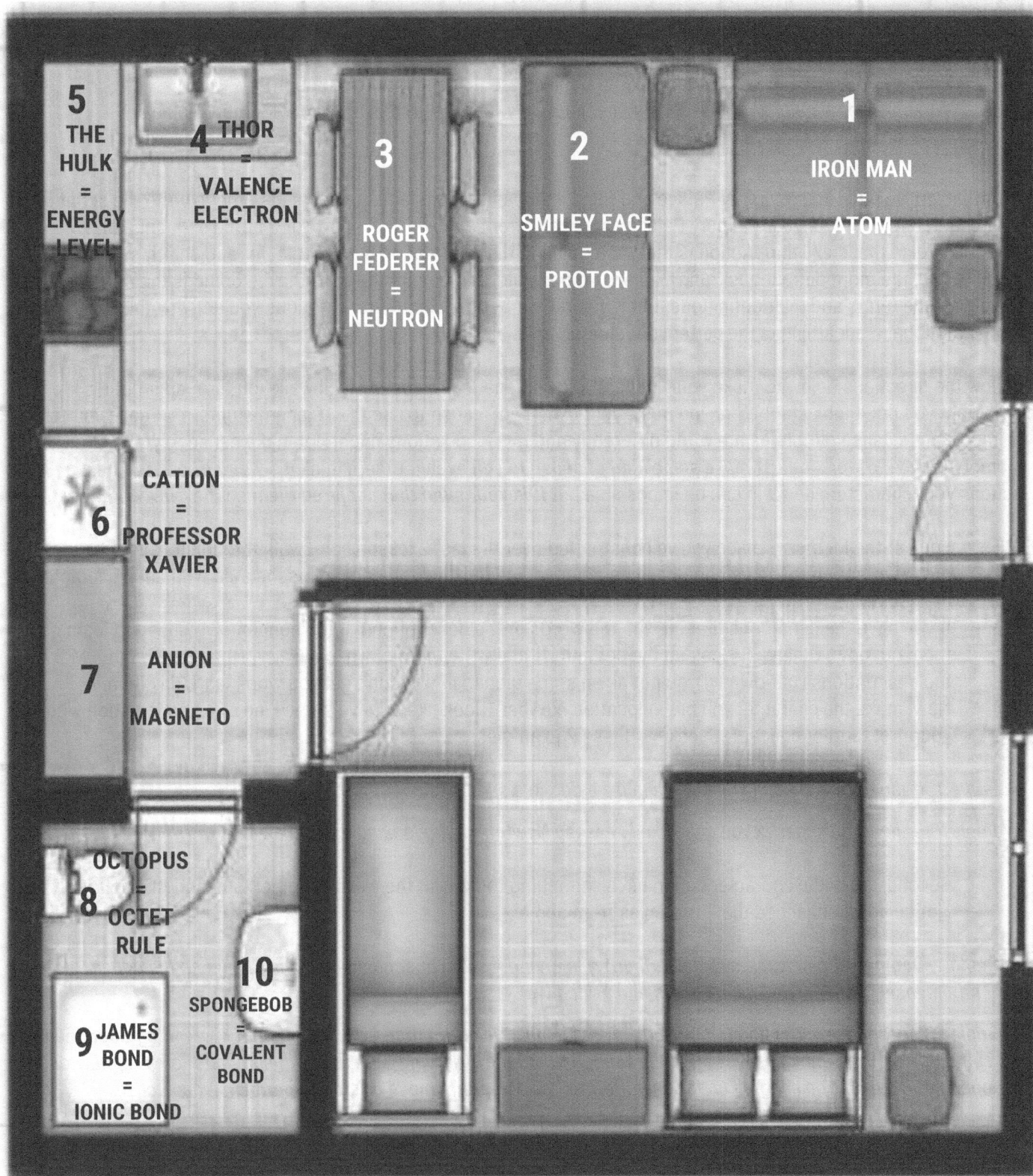

5
THE HULK
=
ENERGY LEVEL

4 THOR
=
VALENCE ELECTRON

3
ROGER FEDERER
=
NEUTRON

2
SMILEY FACE
=
PROTON

1
IRON MAN
=
ATOM

CATION
=
6 PROFESSOR XAVIER

7
ANION
=
MAGNETO

OCTOPUS
=
8 OCTET RULE

10
SPONGEBOB
=
COVALENT BOND

9 JAMES BOND
=
IONIC BOND

If you're like me, you can close your eyes and remember several but not all of your characters, words, and locations in the correct order. Even if you remember all of them right now there's one more thing we must do to imprint all of this information in our brains. We must add action and this part is fun!

LESSON 59 - MAKING MEMORY PALACES MEMORABLE

BIG IDEAS

1. How do you make your Memory Palaces more memorable?
2. Why is it important the characters in your palaces are doing something (action)?
3. What are some quick practice drills you can run in your mind to rehearse your Memory Palaces?

ACTION IT!

Now that you've build your Memory Palace and filled it with characters and concepts it's time to write the script for your characters. Think of your Memory Palace as a scene from a movie like a party or a battle sequence or something else that's exciting. Action is the key to making the information memorable. In fact, and this might seem weird to you, the more outrageous (funny, insane, impossible, and bogus) the stuff they're doing is the better you will remember the terms and their definitions. But if you remember the chapter on emotions you get why this works. The more emotional the learning is the better you remember it.

Follow the directions below to make your "mental" movie. I made one too and will walk you through it but it's important you don't look at it before you make your own if you chose to use the 10 chemistry terms I gave you. This is important because our brains are wired differently and my associations might not make sense to you. For a Memory Palace to work *it must make some kind of sense to you* even if others think it's weird or crazy. Again, actions your characters perform can be impossible but *it is your mind that conjured them* so they will work for you.

1. Look at the Memory Palace you've constructed over the last 2 lessons and walk through it in your head paying attention to the location, the character you added, and the concept associated with each character and location.
2. If you have the definitions that go with the words or the descriptions of the concepts you need to learn get them out now. Otherwise, look up the definitions and write them down in a *way you can understand*. Make the descriptions your own - if you put down some gibberish you don't get you won't learn anything.
3. Now, make the character you put in location number 1 look like or have some kind of an association with your first term or concept. Check out these 2 examples:

*Example 1. If the term is **Dogma** you can visualize a dog in a suit and tie (**authority**).*

*Example 2. If the term is **Inertia** you can visualize **Isaac Newton** (smug-looking dude in a white wig).*

4. Second, make the character action have something to do with the word definition and add this action to it. Notice how I enhanced the 2 examples from above.

*Example 1. **Dogma** - dog in a suit and tie (**authority**) is **giving a speech** standing on his hind legs on the couch (his podium) intensely barking at you his **beliefs and principles**.*

*Example 2. **Inertia** - **Isaac Newton** (smug dude in a white wig) is **alternating between pushing a standing Superman** (in his suit, arms crossed and cape waving in the wind) **and stopping a flying Superman** (in suit, fists forward, Newton wrapped around his ankle hanging on for dear life). He **fails to either move or stop Superman** in each case.*

Notice how detailed the images and the action is. Make it as detailed and vivid as possible. It takes a minute to describe on paper but only a split second to see in your mind. And that's why it works. It's fast but detailed.

5. Repeat for the other terms you have to learn. Write a detailed description for each, similar to the examples. Use the next page to put your visualizations on paper to have an example you can use. In the future, you will be able to easily create new Memory Palaces in your mind alone.

MY MENTAL MOVIE SCRIPT (CHARACTER DESCRIPTIONS & ACTIONS)

1)_____
_____
_____

2)_____
_____
_____

3)_____
_____
_____

4)_____
_____
_____

5)_____
_____
_____

6)_____
_____
_____

7)_____
_____
_____

8)_____
_____
_____

9)_____
_____
_____

10)_____
_____
_____

MY MENTAL MOVIE SCRIPT (MORE THAN 10 TERMS)

11)_____
_____
_____

12)_____
_____
_____

13)_____
_____
_____

14)_____
_____
_____

15)_____
_____
_____

16)_____
_____
_____

17)_____
_____
_____

18)_____
_____
_____

19)_____
_____
_____

20)_____
_____
_____

MY CHEMISTRY MEMORY PALACE EXAMPLE

1. I walk in and see Iron Man sitting on my couch talking and laughing with Smiley Face. On his chest, where the light is, I see the symbol that represents the **atom** and remember that he created an element which is a kind of an atom to save himself before.

2. The yellow Smiley Face is sitting on the sofa vibrating. The weird thing is that in the spots where his eyes would usually be he has plus (+) signs and that's how I know he's the positive particle the **proton**.

3. I keep walking and see the tennis GOAT Roger Federer balancing a tennis ball on his nose. He's from Switzerland - neutral. He's balancing a **neutron**!

4. But why is the God of Thunder Thor hitting the kitchen sink with his hammer? Sparks are flying! Those are **valence electrons** - they have a lot of energy and are the ones reacting to form **bonds**.

5. Suddenly, the green mass of The Hulk jumps off the counter next to Thor and smacks the Asgardian with a club. Thor defends but The Hulk just keeps coming. His **energy level** is unparalleled! Sparks fly - just more **valence electrons** jumping **energy levels**.

6. and   7.   Next to The Hulk and Thor going at it, Professor Xavier and Magneto are using their mental powers to fight it out. They're both mutants - same but different. One is good and one is evil. Xavier is the positive (good) **cation**. Magneto the negative (evil) **anion**.

8. As I walk into the bathroom I get splashed in the face with toilet water. There's an octopus with a crown on his head splashing water joyfully all around with his 8 tentacles. A happy ruler of the toilet, he reminds me of the **octet rule**.

9. To the left of the happy king octopus I see James Bond taking a bubble bath. He's playing with the action figures of Professor Xavier and Magneto. They seem to be friendly though. They stopped fighting and joined forces. Positive and negative form a new friendship, a **bond**. **Cation**? **Anion**? **Bond**? He's the **ionic bond**!

10. This is too much for me. I need to wash my hands. I grab a soap and the sponge. Holy cow! It's Spongebob. That show was always weird to me but I remember that "sharing is caring." Sharing of **valence electrons**. He's the **covalent bond** and my walk is done.

Notice that some terms are used more than once and associated with other terms and meanings. Most of the time, the information you are learning will be somehow connected and you should use those associations when creating Memory Palaces because they will lead to a more complete understanding and better memory.

Chances are some connections my brain made don't make sense to your brain. That's the way it should be. This is why you should make your own.

However, you can use the Memory Palace above to practice visualization. Read each point, close your eyes and picture it. See how quick this is? Use it.

The next page gives you ways to use Memory Palaces effectively and some drills you can use to recall the information they contain. Make it challenging. Make it fun. Learn it.

HOW TO USE MEMORY PALACES

You might have noticed that you started learning the information you put inside your Memory Palace during the process of creating it. You already remember some of the information and you haven't even started using your palace! This is the power of using visual memory and emotions in learning.

Once you learn how to create Memory Palaces you will be able to do it fast. Often, the hardest part is coming up with visuals and associations that go with them. The more you do it the better you'll get at it. Keep at it and the Memory Palace Method will become a tool that will help you learn faster, remember more, and remember longer.

But now, it's time to use your Memory Palace to rehearse the information so you can remember it even when cruelly awakened in the middle of the night and quizzed on it by your friend who forgot the test is tomorrow.

All you have to do is enter your memory palace, walk through it, and observe what the characters are doing. You might need a reminder what some locations were associated with at first, so keep a list of your concepts handy, but don't try to read it over and over to memorize the concepts. Memorizing by rereading doesn't work. Much of the information will never make it to your long-term memory and your understanding will be weak. Build a Memory Palace and do quick practice drills instead.

Practice Drill #1: Walk your Memory Palace forward 2x and then backwards 1x.

Practice Drill #2: Walk your Memory Palace backward 2x and then forward 1x.

Practice Drill #3: Walk your Memory Palace forward 1x, backwards 1x, and then from the middle to the end 2x.

Practice Drill #4: Walk your Memory Palace from the middle to the end 2x and from the middle toward the front 2x.

Practice Drill #5: Forward 1x, backwards 1x, middle in 1x, and middle out 1x.

Practice Drill #6: Create a drill. Make it fun. Do what works for you.

Each drill will take a few minutes and that's all it takes to learn the information if you do 1 drill per day for 5 days straight. Then, you can periodically walk your palace and see that you still remember. It'll be like magic except real.

LESSON 60 - HOW TO CREATE KILLER PRESENTATIONS

BIG IDEAS

1. What are the must have components of effective and engaging presentations?

EXAMINE AN INFOGRAPHIC

Go to *bit.ly/createpres* and examine the *Creating Killer Presentations Infographic*. Take active notes below. Make sure you paraphrase!

Take Notes	Make Notes

SUMMARY:

LESSON 61 - CREATE YOUR KILLER PRESENTATION

BIG IDEAS

1. Practice creating an effective and engaging presentation using the concepts learned in the previous lesson.

APPLY IT! - Create an effective and engaging presentation

Use the must have components you learned about from the ***Creating Killer Presentations Infographic*** (***bit.ly/createpres***) to create a presentation for class, club, team, work etc.

1.   Audience

Who is your audience? _____

What do they like? _____

_____

What do they find boring? _____

_____

How can you use it to make a better presentation? _____

_____

_____

_____

2.   Goal

What is required? _____

_____

What information should you focus on? _____

_____

_____

_____

What do you want to accomplish? _____

_____

_____

_____

3. Reason

What is the reason (or a combination of reasons)? _____

_____

What should you focus on so your presentation reflects the reasons for it?

_____

_____

_____

4. Outline - Most things here should be brief. You are NOT writing the presentation, just planning it. FLIP OVER TO THE SUMMARY PAGE AND WRITE IT FIRST, THEN COME BACK TO THE INTRODUCTION.

Introduction

Complete opening statement (Strong to set the tone. Don't rush on this. Research and write something impactful).

_____

_____

_____

_____

Positive story involving a classmate, teacher etc. (Just name the story - no need to write out the whole thing).

_____

_____

Value (what's in it for the audience?)

_____

_____

Key Points:

1. _____

2. _____

3. _____

4. _____

5. _____

Transition to body _____

Body - Briefly describe, don't write out the whole story/example (example can be a story)

Key Point 1 example _____

_____

Key Point 1 story _____

_____

Transition _____

Key Point 2 example _____

_____

Key Point 2 story _____

_____

Transition _____

Key Point 3 example _____

_____

Key Point 3 story _____

_____

Transition _____

Key Point 4 example _____

_____

Key Point 4 story _____

_____

Transition _____

Key Point 5 example _____

_____

Key Point 5 story _____

_____

Transition to summary _____

Summary - Write this part first, but later practice starting with the introduction.

Restate Key Points

1. _____

2. _____

3. _____

4. _____

5. _____

Transition to close _____

Strong statement (Don't rush on this. Write something inspiring that underlines the importance of your information).

_____

_____

_____

_____

2 examples of how your audience can use what you taught them (brief descriptions).

Example 1. _____

Example 2. _____

Challenge to action (give them the next step they can take in an inspiring but non-threatening way)

_____

_____

_____

_____

Closing statement (Optional if the previous one does the job - you decide)

_____

_____

_____

_____

LESSON 62 - HOW TO PRACTICE FOR A KILLER PRESENTATION

BIG IDEAS

1. Describe an effective way of practicing for a presentation to decrease anxiety and increase success.
2. What are some things to focus on that you normally don't think about?

EXAMINE AN INFOGRAPHIC

Go to *bit.ly/pres_prep* and examine the *How to Practice for a Killer Presentation Infographic*. Take active notes below. Make sure you paraphrase!

Take Notes	Make Notes

SUMMARY:

APPLY IT! - Presentation Practice. Use the drills below to get good at presenting. The more you do it the faster your prep will get in the future because things will occur naturally. But most importantly, YOU WILL KILL when presenting!

PRESENTATION HACK: If you have some down time in class (any class), ask your classmate to watch you present in the hallway (many teachers are cool with it) and give you feedback. Use Drills 1, 2, or 4 below.

Drill #1: Record yourself presenting with your smartphone. Watch it and focus on Speech and Pauses only.

Do you speak clearly?   **Y   N**   Were you loud enough but not too loud?   **Y   N**

How's your pace? **Too fast** ____ **Too slow** ____ **Just right** ____

Did you put emphasis on key points?   **Y   N**   Did you come off natural or forced? _____

Did you pause enough to give the audience time to think or answer rhetorical questions?   **Y   N**

What should you work on? _____

Repeat, making the needed adjustments as many times as you wish. **You're looking for progress not perfection.**

Drill #2: Present to a friend, classmate, family member etc. and ask them to focus on your Body Language.

Do you smile/look like you're enjoying yourself?   **Y   N**   Did you keep eye contact?   **Y   N**

Did your movement and gestures come off as natural or awkward? _____

Explain _____

Did you seem confident or nervous? _____ Explain _____

_____

What should you work on? _____

Repeat, making the needed adjustments as many times as you wish. **You're looking for progress not perfection.**

Drill #3: Visualize yourself giving the presentation. Read the questions below, close your eyes and "see" it all happen in your head. YOU CAN DO THIS DRILL ANY TIME YOU WANT. If you "see" yourself doing the presentation several times before you give it, everything will seem more familiar and calmer. You'll be more confident when it's real.

You stand up. You don't rush. You're confidently taking your time. Where are you standing? How are others seeing you? You take a slow breath and start. You're smiling and confidently going from one key point to another. You notice a person in the audience smiling - it's that encouraging kind of smile. Imagine the teacher (or whoever's in charge) smiling and nodding a lot. The people in the audience are nodding too. You keep moving along giving examples and transitioning. You finish and answer questions. You get sincere and appreciative applause.

Drill #4: Record yourself presenting with your smartphone. Watch it and focus on Speech, Pauses, Transitions, and Body Language. Take notes on the things you need to work on.

REMEMBER: PROGRESS IS PERFECTION

Try not to freak out - it will never be perfect. But trust me, if you practice your presentation will be really, really good (like that sandwich you had the other day you can't stop talking about to your friends good).

LESSON 63 - GIVING KILLER PRESENTATIONS

BIG IDEAS

1. What are the 5 things to pay attention to and do to deliver an impressive and impactful presentation?
2. Explain why presentations are more about "how you say it" and not about "what you say."

EXAMINE AN INFOGRAPHIC

Go to *bit.ly/presgiving* and examine the *How to Deliver a Killer Presentation Infographic*. Take notes (paraphrase).

Take Notes	Make Notes

SUMMARY:

REFLECT - Be honest with yourself and reflect on your past presentations. What are the things you did well? What are the things you should work on?

_____

_____

_____

_____

_____

_____

_____

How can becoming a good presenter/communicator of ideas benefit you in the near and not-so-near future? Think about school, work, and life advantages.

_____

_____

_____

_____

_____

_____

How can investing time in the beginning into learning a skill such as presenting save you time in the future?

_____

_____

_____

_____

_____

LESSON 64 – AVOID "DEATH BY POWERPOINT"

BIG IDEAS

1. What are things you don't want to do when giving a visual presentation?
2. What are the "to dos" of effective slide shows?

WATCH 2 VIDEOS WITH A PARTNER

1. Go to *bit.ly/ppt_death* and watch the *Life After Death by PowerPoint Video*. Take notes on what not to do.
2. Go to *bit.ly/pptbetter* and watch the *How to Avoid Death by PowerPoint Video*. Take notes on THINGS TO AVOID and THINGS TO DO and HOW TO DO THEM when presenting. PAUSE & DRAW EXAMPLES of slides when useful.

EXAMPLES

APPLY IT - Make each of the examples on the left side better. Draw the new and improved slide on the right.

Death By PowerPoint	Life After Death

What's wrong here? _____

_____

_____

What's wrong here? _____

_____

_____

What's wrong here? _____

_____

_____

Explanation of changes _____

_____

_____

Explanation of changes _____

_____

_____

Explanation of changes _____

_____

_____

LESSON 65 - FIND A JEDI MASTER TO TRAIN WITH (LIGHTSABER OPTIONAL)

BIG IDEAS

1. How do you find a mentor who can help you learn and grow faster?
2. How should you approach learning from a mentor?

ACTIVE READING - Read the passage below actively: 1) Preview, 2) Take Notes in the Margins, and 3) Summarize.

{START OF READING}

This is the end of this book but hopefully a new beginning for you. If you got this far and applied what you learned you are a much better student than you were when you started. Isn't is strange how this happens? One lesson makes little difference but combine many little things and you achieve something great. Actually, that's not strange at all. It happens all the time and everywhere in life. The fastest growth happens in small, deliberate, incremental steps like a 2-inch tomato plant in May that grows into a 6-foot tall bush bearing sweet fruit that weighs half a pound in August.

My hope for you is that you can apply the knowledge and the skills you learned and that the fruit of this learning will be success at school, work, relationships, and the rest of your life. Being able to take something and use it, explain it, apply it to something else, change it, reinvent it, and make people's lives (yours included) better in the process is what success is all about, no matter what job or endeavor you partake in. All of those things require the ability to learn effectively. And, the smarter you do it, the faster you can learn new things and master new skills.

But guess what? There's one more thing you can add to your learning arsenal. You can find and train with a Jedi master. Doing this will make learning a specific subject or skill set much faster. Consider this: Luke Skywalker had Obi Wan. The old master helped Luke learn specific Jedi skills and knowledge. Before that, Obi Wan had Yoda do that for him. Later, Luke helped Rey channel the force that awakened within her.

And you can do the same in your life. Think about something you're passionate about. What do you love doing and want to learn more about? It may be something you'd consider as a future profession or side hustle at least. If this is the case and you want to achieve success in it you have but one choice: know more about it and become more skilled in it than most people in this galaxy (or planet at least). To do this, find your Yoda, Obi Wan, or Luke Skywalker and ask them to train you. If one or two individuals in your life fit this profile reach out to them. If you know them well they'll likely be flattered and say yes. Let the training begin!

But let's be real - many of us do not have such a Jedi master - an expert who can train us in our passion field and accelerate our growth in it. However, this may be good news. Research shows that mentoring helps but that informal mentoring is significantly better for growth and success than the business-like type.

How to Find Your Master

Think about your long term goals and dreams. Now, think about the people who inspire you and who you aspire to be more like. This has to be someone prominent. The likes of Mark Cuban, Spike Lee, or Tyra Banks fit the bill if you aspire to crush it in business, film-making, or Reality TV innovation. Decide on an individual who best fits your life and career goals. Then, follow their path and take years off your success climb.

Even Luke Skywalker used books, the Force texts to better grasp the power of the force on his island of solitude. While he was fortunate enough to train with Obi Wan and Yoda these books provided the needed guidance after they departed. This is why Rey saved the ancient books from the fire and took with her.

While watching clever memes and funny panda videos on social media are an enticing entertainment option, these activities contribute little to our personal growth. Your time is better spent learning and the way you learn and what you focus on matters a lot.

Continue reading on the next page →

What to Learn and How

Learn everything you can about your mentor. Go to his or her Wikipedia page and click on each link one by one and read, watch, and listen. Buy every book they wrote or about them and read it. Underline and take notes in each book. Use post it notes or sticky tabs to mark the big a-has. Come back to them often. There's a reason they're at the top of the field you're trying to break into so learn "their way": their thinking, their routines, their process, and their associations.

Devote an entire notebook to learning about this one person and use it to take notes when watching their videos, listening to their podcast appearances, and reading the articles they wrote or were written about them. But most importantly, always reflect on and analyze their thinking and actions. Ask and answer questions such as:

Why did they do it this way?

How did they do it?

What did it accomplish?

How can I apply it?

Learn from their successes and failures. Imitate what works. Avoid what doesn't. In his book **Made in America**, Sam Walton describes visiting competitor's stores to find ideas for his. The billionaire founder of Walmart, seen as a "master" by many, admits he "stole" effective processes from his competitors.

Focus your efforts on this thing alone. Set aside time each day; maybe an hour or two and begin your training. Treat this endeavor as a big project and come up with a plan of study and application. You can use the 3-Step Project Completion Template (***bit.ly/projecttemp***) if you're not sure how to start.

You may the asking: *If this is so easy why doesn't everybody do it?* The truth is that it's not easy. Most people don't have the discipline to study the masters in such a way.

Some people probably find it weird and obsessive - stalker-like. But it's not. Even if you experience feeling creepy about following someone's life journey, the feeling will start fading once you begin noticing the results you're getting. However, consider serious mentor detox if your mind is telling you to move to where they live and start following them around.

Most people never reach the top rungs of the success ladder because they struggle to find the motivation and the willpower to develop success habits, which are ironically the very things you can learn from the masters. Reading one book and watching an occasional video is not enough.

Mastery calls for full immersion and "walking the path" not looking at it from afar. To understand how the master does it, you must examine, analyze, and apply their process. You must fail and learn from it too. The young Skywalker even lost a hand before he could really challenge Darth Vader for Jedi supremacy.

And like Luke, you must find the right path to walk and use its force to achieve mastery. Learn about the force from a master, apply the force repeatedly, and master how to channel the force to accelerate your success.

SUMMARY _____

_____

_____

_____

APPLY IT!

List 1 - 3 things you'd really like to become really good at, do for work in the near future etc. Be bold.

1. _____

2. _____

3. _____

Pick the one thing that is most important to you and list the adults you know well who are experts in this and could mentor you. Don't be afraid to leave this empty - most people will.

_____

List a few prominent (famous, inspiring etc.) people such as sports icons, artists, leaders etc. who are experts in this you could learn from.

_____

Go to their Wikipedia page. Count the number of links (blue) on the page = _____

List 3 books they wrote or were written about them:

1. _____

2. _____

3. _____

Which book will you read first and why? _____

_____

Find 3-5 videos and podcasts they appear in and talk about their journey and their process. Bookmark them on your phone. Which one will you watch/listen to first and why?

_____

_____

What do they create? (physical products like a smartphone, music, videos etc.) List all.

_____

_____

How can you analyze their work to get some insights into their process? Brainstorm.

_____

_____

This is only the beginning - many links are still unexplored. Let nothing stop you. **Keep learning grasshopper.**

PART 3 PROJECT - INFOGRAPHIC

BIG IDEAS

1. What are the 5 strategies from Part 3 you will take with you and use while learning?
2. Why these particular strategies?
3. How do these 5 strategies work and how will they work for you?

THE FINAL PROJECT

Hey. I hope you had fun learning about your brain and the strategies you can use to maximize your brainpower. But while having fun is important it's more important to develop your brainpower into a superpower. Your brain is a supercomputer that runs a program you tell it to run. If the program you run sucks, your brain processing and learning will suck. It's that simple. Feed your brain garbage and it produces garbage.

So what will you feed your brain? Considering this is important because to be successful and fulfilled in life you will have to keep learning all your life. Lifelong learning is a skill that the most successful individuals embrace and live by. Let's take a quick look at highly successful individuals from three different disciplines: technology, music, and basketball.

Bill Gates, Jay Z, or Giannis "The Greek Freak" Antetokounmpo crush it when it comes to their crafts but what they do for a living does not matter as much as what they do with it. If they plan on changing the world by making the lives of everyone around them better and leaving a legacy, they have to keep perfecting their respective crafts. They have to keep getting better. They have to keep learning.

To continue being successful, they have to stay hungry and feed that hunger even when they "retire." In fact, they will never retire. They might change what they do on a daily basis but will continue changing the world in new ways. They will keep learning new things and keep getting better at life. They figured out this is the only way to live a fulfilled life. Making a difference.

But you might say: *Not everyone will become famous so this does not apply to everyone.*

You're right. Not everyone will become famous. But let's consider being a parent. To be a good father or mother you will have to continue to learn about being a good father or mother. As your children grow up they change. If you don't change with them you won't understand them. You won't be able to prepare them for adulthood. Their respect for you might not diminish, but their respect for your opinions will.

Work is the same way. You can keep doing the same 9-to-5 all your life or you can learn and advance. Learning new things and ways to do things in your field will lead to more opportunities. And the quicker and more effectively you can learn, the quicker you can start teaching others. This is what leaders do. They become so good at something it's easy to entrust them with teaching others to do it. Or they strike out on their own.

So...

What will you do? How will you learn? How will you make it more effective?

How will you become so good the world can no longer ignore you?

Flip over for your final project →

FINAL PROJECT - 5 LEARNING STRATEGIES I AM TAKING WITH ME INFOGRAPHIC

1. Create a free account at ***piktochart.com*** and pick a theme to use.
2. Pick 5 learning strategies you learned in Part 3 (Lessons 46 - 65) you found most useful and will continue to use to learn more effectively and be successful in the future.

Strategy 1 _____

Strategy 2 _____

Strategy 3 _____

Strategy 4 _____

Strategy 5 _____

3. Make an infographic in Piktochart. Title it. Organize the 5 strategies in the space provided.
4. In one sentence, explain how each strategy works.
5. Give an example of how or for what someone can use each strategy.
6. Add 1-2 images for each strategy.
7. Put a SUMMARY at the bottom that explains these 3 key points:

1st Point: Where do you plan to use these strategies and what for?
2nd Point: Which particular 1 or 2 strategies do you find most beneficial and why?
3rd Point: How can these strategies help you beyond traditional education?

8. Submit to _____

NOW GO AND CRUSH SCHOOL. THEN CRUSH LIFE.

REFERENCES
1. Focus 2 Achieve - www.focus2achieve.com
2. Jim Kwik Podcast - http://jimkwik.com/category/podcast-1/
3. SPEED READING FOR DUMMIES CHEAT SHEET: http://www.dummies.com/education/language-arts/speed-reading/speed-reading-for-dummies-cheat-sheet/
4. Speed Reading Tips: 5 Ways to Minimize Subvocalization: https://www.irisreading.com/speed-reading-tips-5-ways-to-minimize-subvocalization/
5. He ate all the pi: Japanese man memorises π to 111,700 digits: https://www.theguardian.com/science/alexs-adventures-in-numberland/2015/mar/13/pi-day-2015-memory-memorisation-world-record-japanese-akira-haraguchi
6. How Stephen Curry became the best shooter in the NBA: http://www.businessinsider.com/how-stephen-curry-became-best-shooter-in-the-nba-2015-6
7. How to triple your memory by using this trick: https://www.youtube.com/watch?v=JsC9ZHi79jo
8. Ocean Pollution: 6 Things That Make It Worse: https://www.marineinsight.com/environment/causes-and-effects-of-ocean-dumping/
9. World's largest collection of ocean garbage is twice the size of Texas: https://www.usatoday.com/story/tech/science/2018/03/22/great-pacific-garbage-patch-grows/446405002/
10. The Effectiveness of Mentoring Programs in Corporate Settings: A Meta-Analytical Review of the Literature: https://eric.ed.gov/?id=EJ737832

Made in United States
Cleveland, OH
04 June 2025